The Warfare

Drug Dealer, Drug Addict to Ordained Minister

By

Jan-Dennis Perry

authorHOUSE

1663 Liberty Drive, Suite 200
Bloomington, Indiana 47403
(800) 839-8640
www.authorhouse.com

First published by AuthorHouse 08/12/04

ISBN: 1-4184-7578-5 (e)
ISBN: 1-4184-7579-3 (sc)

Library of Congress Control Number: 2004094238

Printed in the United States of America
Bloomington, Indiana

This book is printed on acid-free paper.

Warfare

The act, the process or an instance of waging conflict, strife or

struggle.

The battle is in your mind.

Table of Contents

Acknowledgements

I would like to dedicate my book first and foremost to Jesus Christ, who is my personal savior. Without Him, none of this would be possible. He is truly the alpha and omega.

I would also like to dedicate this book to my family. A special thanks to my wife Nicole and my two children, Robert and Ayshia. Thanks for standing in the gap for me. I also want to thank my parents, Pastor Luther and Marlena Perry, for always showing me support and love. I also thank my Grandma for being a friend no matter what. I can't forget about my sister Erica L. Perry.

A very special thanks to my wife for writing a chapter in this book. My wife is truly a virtuous woman who is more precious than any ruby.I also want to dedicate this to the Church of God in Christ of Charleston, West Virginia and Friendship Baptist Church, Washington, PA. Thanks for the encouragement.

A special thanks to Pastor Bobby Thomas, Superintendent Bruce E. Hogan, Minister Todd Sharp, Elder Derrick Gibson and Elder Thomas Jackson for all the leadership and guidance, and most of all your friendship. Thanks for your guidance.

A thanks to my greatest two encouragers in the church, Sister Marilyn Lawson and Joanne Beasley.

I also want to dedicate this book to the many families who have had a family member who has been addicted to drugs or alcohol.

I want to let all you guys know that I love and appreciate you.

Preface

This was a confirmation letter written by my pastor, Superintendent Bruce E. Hogan, to my writing of this book. I was torn for such a time about revealing many deep, dark secrets of my life, but I believe that my many tests are a testimony of the many powers and wonders of our Lord and Savior Jesus Christ. We are truly in a spiritual warfare. Things aren't happening by mere chance. My pastor wrote this letter over one year ago; he couldn't find it until the timing was right. It was intended that I be sitting in his congregation to gain the confirmation for this work "The Warfare". Here is the letter:

Where Christ is, hope is being restored and faith becomes an arrow with a target, "Looking unto Jesus, the author and finisher of our faith". The bulls eye is fulfilling the will and purpose of God with our lives, with the ultimate target, the gift of God being eternal life with Him." The mind is the bow, for without the bow the arrow lays motionless and the target stands waiting. Therefore I stand and cry out, "Cast the devil out of my mind!"

As a part of God's body with an understanding in regards to the real spiritual warfare that the Christian confronts daily, our objective is to embrace God's will in our lives. Our calling is to bring relevance back to holiness, sanctification, the true purpose of faith, and to preach and teach God's word, not handling the Word of God deceitfully as some, which have caused a spiritual drought in our land.

As our country, one of the greatest in the world, experiences a war of a different kind, the Christian body, and many members fitly joined together, must be a warring church. If you do not wrestle against powers and principalities, against the rulers of darkness of this world, and spiritual wickedness in high places, "you will not prevail the onslaught of false doctrine, compromise, and powerlessness in this wicked generation". The Gospel of Jesus Christ is the good news, setting the captive soul free, indeed persuaded that neither death, nor life, nor angels, nor principalities, nor power, nor things to come… shall be able to separate you from the love of God.   This is not a mere intellectual experience nor an emotional high found in a blind emotional frenzy that has no ability to impart a real change in a person's life; this goes beyond a dance, and a tambourine and another discussion of how it used to be and past spiritual victories! It is time for war! Many have become disillusioned by the routine of church as usual on Sunday and realize that it is a time for war!

God is calling His people to know Him in the power of His resurrection, intimately, and not merely standing outside of the inner courts only observing His presence from a great distance through religious traditions and rituals. In fact, Christian living is only effective through successful disciplining. Write the vision and make it clear, a vision of Christians actively involved in evangelism, reaching out in the home, community, nation, and the world, disciplining men and women who in turn will disciple others. Oh that we will be found disciples, standing as we behold the testing times of confrontation and judgment that is to come, and yet already is.

Preaching (how can you hear without a preacher) and teaching can not just be doctrinal, but must be preached and taught as relevant for our times as it relates to what God is doing today, not only what He has already done. "Mere words profit nothing," it is the anointing of God through the Spirit of God that opens the heart to receive the Truth.

"It is imperative for change that we confront our doubts, fears, strongholds, traditions, sins, excuses, and the like, and receive the yoke destroying life changing power of Jesus Christ which will liberate and purge us from dead works so we can go on to perfection fulfilling the call and purpose God has given to each person." "For I know the thoughts that I think toward you, saith the Lord, thoughts of peace and not of evil, to give you an expected end." *Jeremiah 29:11*

Your soul can rest, and your flesh put in check! Focus not on membership, but discipleship.

Foreword

I truly know how God can turn a person's life around. The book tells parent's how the devil is trying to still our children. He almost got me. But thank God, I called upon his name, and he answered my call. I want every man, woman and child to know that Christ can do the same for them. No matter what the situation is God can turn it around for their good. He took me from being a drug dealer to a drug addict to now a Minister in God's house. I want you to know that he can do the same for you. The bible tells us in Romans 10:9 That if thou shall confess with thy mouth the lord Jesus, and shalt believe in thine heart that God hath raised from the dead, thou shalt be saved. Yes we can be saved from addiction and any other oppression that the devil has put upon us. I'm here to let you know that the devil may be mighty but Jesus is Almighty. The real warfare is in your mind. .It is in the mind that the battle takes place.

Introduction

Dear heavenly Father, I humbly bow before you giving You thanks for Your direction and Your strength. I have endured as a good soldier and this is my testament. If it had not been for You this work would not be possible; with the renewal of Your grace and mercy I have overcome! Amen.

I start with an announcement to the devil, Satan, himself. I want you to know I am calling you out in the name of Jesus. You are a liar; as a matter of fact you are the father of all lies. You meant from the onset of time for me to fail, but you forgot I had Jesus in my corner. I thank you Jesus for leaving me the deed and title to all your promises. I thank You for leaving your last will and testament for it is written that I was predestined to inherit the goodness of the land!

The purpose of this book is to let those who have fallen to know that they can get up.

Drugs and alcohol have affected almost every home in America. It is the devils trap; he puts thoughts of failure and discontentment in our minds. He declares war on our very existence. For those of you who have had someone fall prey to substance abuse, or any other obstacle in life; I want you to help the person get back up on his or her feet. Jesse Jackson once said, "Never look down on a man, unless you are helping them up." The Bible says that we are to have mercy, as a matter of fact, it is written, blessed are the merciful for they shall obtain mercy! I need you to understand that anything written by God is a contract that cannot be broken, so don't believe the "hype", if you have fallen get up!

I have had an extraordinary journey throughout my life, not knowing where the journey would end until I accepted Jesus Christ as my personal savior. I have been writing this book for over three years, not knowing that I was in the middle of a war. I have been in a battle in my mind. I'm starting my story somewhere in the middle of my life because that's when the major confrontation took place, although the devil started laying the ground work, years ago. The devils main goal was to prevent me from preaching and teaching the Gospel of Jesus Christ. I don't know where this path in life may take me, but I now know that my destination is heaven. I can't wait to sit in heaven with my new robe at my master's feet, just enjoying His magnificent presence. I can't wait to meet some of my heroes, Peter, Paul, John the Baptist David and many others. I can't wait to tell Job how much I admired his courage through all his atrocities, but most of all I can't wait to hear the Lord say, "Well done, my good and faithful servant."

My story starts September 14, 1968 at St. Mary's Hospital in Clarksburg, West Virginia. This is where I was born the son of Luther D. and Marlena A. Perry. I grew up under the leadership of a Christian family. See, my father is the

Reverend Luther D. Perry. I had a decent childhood, although at times it is mighty rough to grow up a preacher's kid; often we're known as "PKs". I also have a sister, Erica Lynn Perry. She is quite a bit younger than me. She won't have much of a part in my story, probably because she learned the do's and don'ts in life by the bad example that I set for her. I only hope that my life today is an example for her to live by. If I only knew then what I know today I could have prevented a lot of the trials I endured. I guess that's where we get the old cliché that hindsight is 20/20.

It wasn't so bad growing up as a preacher's kid , but at the time I thought it was awful. The stresses of being a PK are almost unbearable the criticism from other kids, always having to be perfect. I always felt like all eyes were on me. I had to sing in the choir when I didn't want to or even like to sing. I guess some of these things must sound petty to you, but it adds up. I think the worst thing about being a PK was never having my father that is, my paternal father all to myself. When other dads were watching their sons play sports or playing sports with their sons, my dad was always preaching, visiting the sick or tending to some need of a church member. I guess it's kind of selfish when I look back on it because a preacher has a job more important than the president of the United States. A preacher is responsible for our souls. Now, I don't want you to think my parents were bad people because they did spend some quality time with me. I realize my father did the best he could. He was always a good role model and provider. I just never really got to know him and be his friend. I know I haven't said much about my mother, but she was like a mother and father figure to me. We were friends, but she always had to have everything in order. She never took time to sit down and just get to know me for who I was. It seemed as if she was always on the go. I thank God for them both. Later on in my story, you'll see some amazing love from these two people. I'm just giving you a little background from the eyes of a kid who didn't know much about the world and knew even less about divine life.

As I begin to get into the meat and potatoes of my life, you'll see what unconditional love is and what it means. You will also see that I didn't realize that they were instilling character, courage and morals that I would need later on in life as I began to have a battle with the gates of hell and the devil himself. I'm going to give you a little more history of my early childhood and then I'm going to tell you about being a PK teenager, which will prepare you for my journey from drug dealer to drug addict to ordained elder. I really grew up like other normal African-American teenagers. I guess you could even say that I had more advantages than the social norm. I had two married parents who were Christians; we were a middle class family. That didn't stop the devil. I didn't know that I was in the midst of a spiritual battle that began the day I was born.

Chapter One
The Wonder Years

I guess all of my troubles started during my teenage years. Most teenagers look back and call them the wonder years, but I call them the temptation years. I believe your teenage years are the first fork in the road. I'll elaborate a little bit. This is the time when you know right from wrong, but you have to make a choice while traveling down life's path. Do you take the road less traveled, or do you take the popular road? What a decision to have to make between the ages of thirteen and fourteen. Hard to believe, isn't it parents, but this is about the age when your kids start getting into everything from alcohol, sex and drugs to, yes, even becoming a drug dealer and drug addict, a common thug! When I was in the eighth grade, I was introduced to drinking. It was the cool thing to do. We would go out as little boys and hustle the local winos to buy us a bottle of Boones Farm Tickle Pink. It's hard to imagine, but an eighth-grade boy or girl hustling a grown man. I've come to realize today that we weren't hustling the wino but preying on his weakness. He was an alcoholic. He would do about anything for that drink. I never became that wino that I made fun of, but I became something worse   a drug addict and alcoholic who would do anything for that quick fix. This is how the devil's trap starts. Believe me, he has caught many good men and women through his lies and deceit. I just thank God that I was blessed to survive to tell my story because many others weren't. We didn't think we were hurting anyone, but we were putting garbage into God's holy temple. In the first book of Corinthians, sixth chapter and nineteenth verse, the bible tells us Know ye not that your body is the temple of the Holy Ghost which is in you, which ye have of God, and ye are not your own. I already had some direction from the manual of life, which is the Bible, but I was too young and foolish to realize. Every once in a while in the book, you'll notice I'll back up some of the lessons with scripture. I'll do this to honor and glorify my holy Father and also to show you that the Lord has an instruction manual for us to live by.

Now, back to the story. Soon after hustling the wino to buy us Tickle Pink, we were drinking with him before we would go into the skating rink. The rink was our favorite place to drink. Our parents would drop us off there and think that we were supervised, but this was just a rink of sin, a place to meet other unsaved teenagers who were experimenting with everything from drinking to drugs to having their first sexual encounters. As I was saying before, we were now to the stage of drinking with the wino. (Sometimes you'll hear me refer to "we" in the book; I'm talking about some of my teenage peers. I won't name in the book due to confidentiality.) We had even begun to drink what he was drinking Mad Dog 20/20, Wild Irish Bird and, "what's the word", Thunderbird. We would even have the brown bag wrapped around it. During my skating rink days I experienced a traumatic first in my life. It was lying to my parents. I used to think that my first "real" lie to them was this: One night I came home from the rink sloppy drunk and I was going to do my normal routine and run quickly up to my bedroom and go to sleep. This time, I ran into my dad in the hallway. He asked me what that smell was on me. He asked me if I was drinking. I told him my first face-to-face lie. As a matter of fact, I got so nervous I threw up right in front of him. He never said a word that night. He waited until I was good and sick the next morning. Then he came and got me. He made me clean up the vomit from the night before; I guess he was hoping this would somehow teach me a lesson. I didn't realize it at the time, but this wasn't my first lie to my parents. I had been lying all the time. Each time they trusted me to go to the skating rink and use the moral values that they had instilled in me, I lied. I did the exact opposite. The next traumatic event that happened to me at the rink was one night when a good friend of mine was killed. He had come into the rink that night for a little while, but left with some girls from Grafton, West Virginia. They were drinking heavily and were in a car accident. It is rumored that they were thrown out of the car and that one of the female passengers was decapitated. This is what drinking and driving will do to you. We were in the rink at this time with not a care in the world, until the music stopped playing and an announcement came over the intercom telling us about the accident. Later the next day, my friend died. He was one of the greatest football talents ever, but the devil was able to prevent him from using his God-given talent. Right then, I should have seen what drugs and alcohol could do to a person's life. It should have taught me that living out of God's will gives the devil an opportunity to rear his ugly head. The devil only has three purposes in a person's life. They are to kill, steal and destroy a person's life or joy of life. After all the drama I saw going on in my teenage years, I kept right on living the fast life. I saw and did many wicked things. It was as if I were living in a teenage Sodom and Gomorrah. There was teenage sex going on all around me. I became sexually promiscuous at an early age. I saw young men use one young lady after another. We would switch partners like they used to do in the 1960s. I didn't realize that I was building a life that would later come back to haunt me. I knew this behavior was wrong, but it wasn't enough to open my eyes. Instead, I kept building a foundation for Satan to creep into my life and almost destroy it, if it weren't for the loving mercy of God. I've skipped some details during my teenage years. I just wanted to show you some major building blocks on my journey from drug dealer to drug addict to Elder .. I just to let shed some light for some teenager out there, or let his or her parents know how easy it is to let Satan steal your life. It can happen within a blink of an eye. Don't start at an early age building a foundation for destruction, do not let Satan destroy your life before you have an opportunity to live it. If you serve God and surround yourself with other Christians, you will be building a foundation on solid ground. This means that when trials and tribulations come later in life, you will be able to weather the storm. If, early in life, you learn to deal with your life through drinking, drugging and having sex, you'll be building your foundation on sand. You won't know how to live life on life's terms. Sand is easy to blow away, you need a solid foundation to stand on; do not be deceived. If you don't start building your foundation early, your house will fall down. This doesn't mean that we won't have some failures in life, because we will. What it means is that we will be able to deal with all of life's situations with rational thinking. You need to know that you may have to take the hard road, a less traveled road, but you can endure. It's not easy being a Christian, especially as a teenager, but it's a lot easier than living a life of confusion and turmoil. I didn't realize in my teenage years all of the opportunities I missed while using mood-altering substances. I could have been valedictorian of my class. I could have been an exceptional football player and, more than anything, I could have been one of the greatest soldiers for Jesus Christ. This brings to memory my high school athletic career. It could have been something extraordinary, but instead, I often found myself watching, drunk on the sideline. I couldn't understand why so many of my coaches and teachers would tell me that I had all of the potential in the world. I just wouldn't use it. A couple of instances stick out in my mind in high school sports. One was my football career I was a starter from my freshman year. One Friday night, I was playing against Grafton High School and I was having the game of my life. I was leading the team in tackles, yardage and special teams. Now imagine what kind of game I could have had if I weren't drunk, and I mean sloppy drunk. I was so drunk and disoriented at halftime, I had to take a shower to sober up. I remember another incident in high school was the Harrison County track meet. This was a bad time for me to have a track meet , because it would interfere with me drinking on senior skip day. I went out during one of the most important track meets of the year and got so drunk that my ride wouldn't take me home. I was puking my guts out, and my so-called friend with whom I had been drinking was willing to leave me stranded out in a wooded area where a black man had no business in the first place. My father had to come and get his sloppy-drunk teenage son. What an embarrassment I must have been to him. Remember, he was a man of God. He was a pastor of a local church, and his son was a teenage wreck. He never told me that I was an embarrassment, but I always felt that I must have been. This was my conscience talking to me. I didn't realize that then. Even though I was a disgrace, he still took me to the track meet. This is where I ran the worst race of my life. I never will forget how I embarrassed myself as an athlete that day. I ran the 400-meter relay. I started the race like I was running the 100-yard dash   I actually thought I was running the 100, if the truth be known. I took about a 100-yard lead on everybody in the race, and when I got halfway through I couldn't finish the race. I was too drunk. I was reeking of alcohol but still didn't realize that most kids my age wouldn't get sloshed before such an important event. This is a primary example of how sin; can keep you from finishing the race of life.   Sin has caused many a good man or woman to loose sight of life's finish line. Back then; I thought life was a joke. Instead, I slipped through the system by just being average or at least what I thought was average. As a matter of fact, I never even gave myself a chance to figure out who I really was. I became what other people wanted me to be. I could adapt to any situation by becoming a "yes" man. I would say yes to whatever the crowd wanted to do. I was a coward. I wouldn't stand up for what was right or what my parents had instilled in me. Instead, I took the frequently traveled road, the one that I thought was the road with less heartache. If you continue reading this book, you'll find out that there was plenty of heartache to come. As a matter of fact, you'll find out that I'm writing this book in the midst of a storm. I didn't realize that I was creating a pattern for myself. See, for most of my life I have been making terrible decisions   that is, until I accepted Jesus Christ as my personal savior. Even though my life has changed today, I still have to face some of those heartaches that I caused my family and myself from my past living. Today as I write in my book, I just got news that I have been indicted for robbery in the second degree. Thank God, that when I turned my life over to Him that my old life was dead and a new creature was born. The world will try and hold you accountable for your sinful life, but Jesus has already paid the price, through his death, burial and resurrection. . My life has truly been a process. It has made a 180-degree turn. My teenage years were the foundation that I had built for my life to take some of the turns that it has taken. After high school, my sinful life went to the next level, especially during my college years. All those bad habits I learned during my early teenage years, I took to the next level. I started college at seventeen years of age. I went to Marshall University in Huntington, West Virginia. This should have been the best time of my life. In fact, this should have been my wonder years. This was my first taste of complete freedom away from my parents. No more hiding the inner demon that I had lurking deep in my inner being.

Instead of learning knowledge from my professors, I learned from the thugs, drug dealers, pimps and prostitutes. I learned to hustle. College started out pretty fun. I even had good grades like a normal college student in my first couple of years. I did make some pretty good friends. You could say I even met my first wife during this period. Her name was Marie. You'll hear more about her a little later. On my first day of college, I met some key players in my life, two of my best friends, Kendell and Roger. I don't even talk to them today. I don't know where Kendell is the last I heard, he was somewhere in Columbus, Ohio, fighting his own demons. Roger is in federal prison serving a twenty-year sentence for kingpin drug charges. It's a shame; he has a master's degree from Marshall University. We were educated thugs, but obviously not very smart.. I hope they don't mind me mentioning them, but they are a big part of what I had become .

I still love the two of them as if they were my own brothers. My prayers are that one day we will all be brothers in Christ Jesus. I hardly know how to stay on track when I talk about those days. All I know is that I would give anything to do those days all over again. Who knows? The three of us might have been very important men in society, maybe even three Christian men running a major corporation, doing good things for the black community, instead of being statistics, but I do have to let you in on some good news, which is the gospel, Joshua said that "the devil meant it for bad, but God meant it for good" Our testimonies are meant to prevent some young or old person from self destruction.

When I started college, I lived in Twin Towers East, the men's dormitory. This was like one great big party. I had already learned how to do just enough to get by in high school; , although I was pretty intelligent. The first year of college was like a big orgy. All I did was sleep from woman to woman, lie and cheat. I thought this is what normal college students did. I didn't know that my body was infested with the disease of addiction. I guess where I got my street degree was in the inner city of Huntington. I had started pledging a fraternity my second semester of college. (Kappa Alpha Psi Fraternity, Inc. Yes, I'm a Nupe.) This was where I started hanging out in the streets. It's a funny thing about the streets   it will take you in like you're one of it's own. Then it will crush you. It is like an old saying I always hear my pastor say that the devil says, "Have anything you want be cause you're paying anyway." When I was in the streets, I learned all kinds of tricks. I learned that if I sold marijuana, I could smoke it for free. It would also pay for my beer, wine and liquor. It was also a great way to keep plenty of ladies around. I didn't know it then, but I was already addicted to the power I felt when I was controlling people's lives.

Chapter Two
The Interracial Marriage and Divorce

I would have to say that this next chapter is where my problems actually began . It is a tale of romance, love, betrayal, adultery and physical and mental abuse. It is the story of an interracial marriage and the difficulties that come with such a decision. All of the habits that I acquired during my teenage years were just building blocks for the drastic turn of events in my life. I met and later married a young lady named Marie.. I had seen her many times before I actually met her. The day that I met her changed my life forever. Somehow, what I thought was the best day of my life would continue to haunt me for the next ten years. I never will forget our first encounter. I was at the mall with a couple of my friends. I saw her in the mall parking lot. We were at the Fireman's fair, which was taking place at the mall. The thing I remember most about her were her eyes. There is something about a person's eyes that should give you a clue to what lies within their soul. I would like to think so anyway. After seeing her briefly I knew she would one day be my wife. I know that is far fetched, but that is how I felt, and I was going to make her my wife. It was like the forbidden fruit in the Garden of Eden. Here was a young rich Caucasian girl, who wasn't suppose to be dating an African American. It became a challenge, and I love a good challenge. .

Soon after meeting her, we started a slow courtship. . It was very difficult, a young prominent white girl dating a black male in a small community. This is a difficult task in itself. Although, it seems more acceptable today, you will still find many people who believe you should not date outside your race. There were so many obstacles. and I know that those obstacles are what drew us together. A lot of parents don't realize that they can add fire to a relationship just by opposing the relationship. . It somehow made the relationship exciting, defying the wishes of our parents., sWe would have to sneak around and hide our relationship from almost everyone. That should have been a wake up call that there was trouble lying ahead; but love is blind and you couldn't see the truth if it was staring you in the face, nor would you want to see it. . This is why it is very important that you do not unequal your yokes. Let me explain, I was raised in a Christian household, and I was pursuing someone who was not raised in the same setting. We were wrong for each other from the beginning. As the old saying goes, we always want what we are not suppose to have, or what isn't good for us. We often had to be very creative to see each other. This added stress to our relationship, but still we decided to pursue it anyway. We would go stay with friends when their parents were out of town. It seemed like we were in a fairy tale sometimes, but the truth of the matter is that we were in sin from the onset. I often tried to lavish her with gifts and fine dinners, although I was really no competition with what her wealthy father was providing for her. I somehow thought I was showing her love, but actually manipulating the relationship into something perceived as "normal". were Facing all the opposition to our interracial dating drew us closer together. We were not only companions, but also co-conspirators in this game of manipulation. We not only deceived ourselves, but everyone we came in contact with. . I didn't realize it at the time that we only had a few things in common.

Most of our relationship was based on other people's prejudice and hate. We spent the majority of our dating career finding ways to be together. Now, I do have to admit that I did love her. As a matter of fact, losing her was one of the most painful experiences that I have ever felt. . I never did realize that I didn't really get to know her as an adult. I only knew her as a child with a terrible secret. I won't go into all the details, but her family didn't like me very much because of the color of my skin. Sometimes when I think about the situation today, I think Marie was trying to rebel against her parents. I don't really know if that was the case, but. I would like to believe that we truly loved each other once. It started out romantically. I thought that this would be the relationship that would last until my final day, but how mistaken had I been. I would meet her in places that no one would ever imagine. For example, in the middle of the baseball field after the park had closed to share a meal. . We would often have picnics in the park or meet in a hotel. We would sometimes meet at my parents' house. They seemed to like her or feel sorry for her. Like I mentioned earlier, her parents, especially her dad, did not approve of our relationship . The more her parents would try and drive a wedge between us, the closer we became, especially when I went away to college. If her parents weren't so determined to break us up, college might have separated us, but then again maybe not. She was a beautiful woman and I was proud to have her as mine.. My college friends all thought she was a nice looking young lady.

I was really too young to be this head-over-heels about one girl, but it seemed like I couldn't live without her. Now, I was telling you earlier that we had to sneak around a lot. This worked out well when I went to college. She would tell her parents that she was spending the night with a friend, and she would come spend the entire weekend with me at college. It also worked out for me because I was living a double life. I was the good boyfriend when she was around but a whoremonger when we were apart. We both had a lot of secrets. It was a double life for both of us. I was behaving in such a manner and claiming to be in love with someone I couldn't be without. That should let you know I was not thinking rationally, nor mature enough to know accept reality. Some people may describe individuals of this nature as players. (A player was someone who partied all the time, someone who kept many women, booze, drugs and money.) Marie never realized any of this cause I would become a totally different person around her. Now on the other hand, she was a typical rich white girl who happened to fall in love or lust with a black man. I had often heard rumors of her dating and calling other men, but I overlooked it. I now realize I never pursued those feelings because I felt guilty about my own discretions . She would tell me that the rumors weren't true and I would believe her. How could I question her when I was doing the same things that I was questioning her about?

I look back now and believe that we both had been caught up in the idea of dating outside our race. . I also believe that we both wanted to defy all the odds. During my junior year in college, the summer of 1987, we decided to get married. I was getting older and couldn't stand sneaking around anymore. Even our wedding ceremony caused conflict. Her father refused to come to the wedding. My parents were controlling we were even pressured as to where we would get married. We wanted to be married at Mount Zion Baptist Church , but my parents made me feel obligated to get married at the church where my father was the pastor. . I did not want to get married there, but I did not want to offend my father either. Today I have learned that you cannot please everyone. . In life, you have to do what is best for you. . We got married and thought we could make it on love. I've got news for anyone endeavoring in an interracial marriage; the world is a cruel place with some evil people. So, if you decide to take on the challenge of an interracial relationship, have God in the midst. The odds were stacked against us in every possible way. We were young and jobless, with no formal education, and one of us was black and the other white. Even today I don't have anything against interracial marriages, but you better make sure that God has a part in it. You will need God's help to endure the cruelties of this world. Marriage is a sacred thing. It's not an easy endeavor. It's hard enough to be married to someone of the same race who understands your history and culture. Marriage is something that a couple has to work at constantly. I just believe that, with all the hardships black people face, it is even more difficult if you are a black male trying to make it in a predominantly white society with a white woman on your arm. You can look at all the black celebrities married to Caucasians, and see that statistics show that most interracial marriages end in divorce.. . . It's just a difficult situation. One of the main reasons that marriages fail, whether interracial or not, is not having God as the foundation.

After Marie and I were married, we went to live in the marriage dorms in Huntington. Things started out pretty well. It was like playing house, until all of the adult duties came into play. It was also difficult when we would go to visit my parents. We would never get to go to her parent's home who were only minutes away. Her mom would sometimes sneak over to my parents' house and visit with her daughter Her father resented the mere thought of us being married. This is exactly what I am speaking of when I say interracial marriages have many obstacles to endure and overcome.

I worked nights at United Parcel Service and went to school during the day. Marie also worked and went to school full time. That's one thing I will say about her she was always a hard worker. As a matter of fact, she had a lot of good qualities. We got along well for a while that is, until there weren't any more obstacles or confusion to face in the relationship.. I now realize that we didn't really know each other. We were thriving on the challenges of staying together, and now we could be somewhat "normal", and all hell broke loose. It was like forbidden fruit in the Garden of Eden and we both had our taste. Now, what is to come of our love and life together?

After the first year of marriage, some of those habits that we had hidden from each other had began to surface. . It's sort of like that old saying that you don't really know a person until you live with them. I was a borderline alcoholic the whole time, especially on the weekends. I was also an occasional weed smoker who would often buy a bag and break it down so I could smoke for free. ("Break it down" means to buy an ounce of weed and break it down into ten-dollar sacks of weed. I could buy an ounce for $150 back then and get about twenty-five ten-dollar bags out of it.) The whole time we dated, Marie didn't have a clue that I drank so much or that I ever smoked weed, much less sold it sometimes. As the year went on, I began to coerce her to start drinking and sometimes smoke a joint. I could tell she really didn't approve of any of these habits, so I would often sneak and indulge myself. I have to admit, looking back, that I did drink and party a lot more than I realized. I was just like any other alcoholic and addict. I was in a state of denial. Now Marie had some habits of her own, like excessive spending. She was high maintenance. Who could blame her, though? She was a young, rich white girl who was used to having anything her heart desired. This went on for a while. What happened next sets the basis for my story: "Drug Dealer, Drug Addict to Ordained Minister". It's one of the reasons you're reading my story today.

I know I had some habits that drove her away, but I truly never dreamed that we wouldn't be together. I never realized that this lady had become a part of me, and that I once loved her. I just had some problems with alcoholism, addiction and maturity. Remember, in the beginning I told you that I had picked up some bad habits that would be building blocks to my life. As time went on in my marriage, I became very controlling. I would go out during the day after school and drink with the old men at UPS. It reminds me of when I was a young teen drinking with the winos outside the skating rink. I didn't realize that I was mentally abusing Marie. I would feel inadequate sometimes and make up things about her. I would tell her that she was ugly or that she had some sort of flaw. It wasn't true. She was beautiful, but not as beautiful as the woman the Lord has given me today.. I thought I should clear that up right now. Even though I'm just reflecting on my past, I don't want to sleep on the couch now. Yes, I'm remarried now to the most beautiful woman in the entire world. I'll tell you about her later in the book, so keep on reading and you'll hear about true love and friendship. Back to my inadequacies.

That's what people often do who aren't happy with themselves. At least that's the way I was. I appeared confident, but inside I was a lonely, frightened little boy. Marie had gotten tired of the mental abuse and decided to make decisions that would haunt me for a long time. I never saw it coming; one Saturday I got off work early as we had plans to attend a football game. , . . I never will forget that morning; it was actually the last civil day I ever spent with Marie.

At the time, I never knew it would be the last time we would ever be civil towards one another. You never know how a person's life can change in the twinkling of an eye. When I went to work, it appeared that everything was fine in our relationship. I didn't know that she had secrets, too. That day at work my truck broke down and I got to go home early. My wife at the time was nowhere to be found. As a matter of fact, she didn't come home till about 4:00 in the morning. When I went to question her about where she'd been, she blew up. (This was one of my old tactics create a fight so that I could leave again.) That is exactly what she did she left. I never had a clue that she had another man all this time. I was betrayed. I found out that Marie had plenty of secrets of her own.

To this day, I don't know how many of the rumors are true or not true. I would like to think some of the most terrible stories aren't true. The one story that I do know is true is that this woman I loved and trusted was having an affair with a basketball player. This was only the beginning; I found out that she had been seeing him for quite a while. She not only had an affair with a player, but one of the rumors was that she was seeing the coach also. This tore my heart right out of my chest. We were getting a divorce. It was a messy divorce. It seemed like we stayed in court. She would often accuse me of stalking her. This wasn't true at all I really did not want to see her again. When she left me, I had no idea where she was living. It just happened that the apartment she lived in was an apartment that my friend Roger dealt drugs from. I would go over to his apartment and play cards and drink my misery away. I didn't know she lived there until one morning I was coming out of Roger's and I happened to look up and see her and the basketball player embracing. My friend Roger saved both of their lives that day. I was carrying a whop with me that morning. (A whop is a Mac 10 sub caliber machine gun.) I had just won it in a card game off of Roger. If he hadn't been coming out of the house behind me, they would have been dead and I would have been writing this book from prison. He tackled me and took the gun from me. I tried to get the man Marie was with to come down off the porch, but he wouldn't. I then recognized his car. I realized that his car had been parked outside my house before. I would often see this little red car as I would pass my house. I would be in the UPS truck. I lived on the same road where I worked. I worked the night shift and would pass my house on the way to Lexington, Kentucky. As I realized that I had seen this car before, I became enraged. . When he wouldn't come down to fight with me, I began to taunt and ultimately damage his car. . .

I realize today what comes around goes around. All of the seed that I had sowed in the dark was now at full bloom. It was my time to harvest. I did pay; I paid double, maybe even triple. To this day, we have never sat down and talked. I still find that strange. To sum up the demise of my marriage, it sets the stage for my days as a drug dealer. I was looking for happiness; , I was looking for a way just to escape the tragedy that was going on in my life. It was bad enough that I had separated from my first love, but how could this person I loved bring so much torment and pain to my life I will tell you how, in just one word from the bible, sin! You have to be careful in life that your partner is who God destined you to be with. You both should be in sync with God and one another. God gives you the foundation for a successful, rewarding marriage. One should know and seek the Lord first. I thank God for interceding and saving me for my predestined wife.

? My marriage had come to an end, but the streets adopted me. . I know today that it was the devil and his many spirits lurking all around and waiting to take me in. They were waiting for an opportunity to use me and destroy me. The devil needs a body to use. If he doesn't have a body, it's hard for him to operate. He had been setting traps and pitfalls my entire life, you see he had a plan for me too, and I didn't even realize it. The devil began to talk to me; he told me how I could find power and love by selling drugs He put thoughts into my mind that weren't even mine. That is the way he operates. The battle is in your mind and he utilized my pain and need for love to began a all out attack on my life. I tried to escape losing my wife by staying drunk or high on drugs. He showed me that I could control people, especially women, through drugs and money. Every time I would start to feel bad, he would give me another rumor about Marie that I couldn't handle. This is how Satan operates, he needs a witness to carry on his lies and deceit. It was hard to bare hearing such fowl things about a woman I once loved, and at this point probably still loved. Please be mindful of this when you began to speak something you know is false or damaging.As you continue to read take note of the mental battles I have endured due to the backlash of this failed marriage. These battles are pertinent to the onset of my drug addiction, There are many precursors to the problems that I have endured, that is why I must stay focused on where God has brought me to today. The devil wants us to look back on the things of our past that seemingly felt good to us at the time, but he doesn't show the good with the bad, he only shows the good. He often confuses our perception with reality. As I would have these flashbacks, as I sometimes call them. I can remember the good times I had with my first wife, but I felled to see the lies, infidelity, deceit and turmoil that came with that relationship. I know to never look back on any situation that God has delivered me from. To this day, Marie has never told me in person what happened I only have the devils version. I don't know what drove her out of my life? I can only speculate. I would have to say it was a collaborate endeavor from both of us. I wish not to blame anyone for my faults and shortcomings. I take full responsibility for my role in the demise of my first marriage.

I guess where my heart really got hard was when I started praying to God for help and I didn't hear Him respond. At least He didn't respond like I wanted Him to. I didn't realize that my prayers were blocked, that I needed to ask God for forgiveness for my own transgressions and that I needed Him, He didn't need me. I was too busy listening to the devil. My mind was altered with drugs, alcohol and women. I was looking for comfort in all the wrong places. I needed help to deal with what was going on in my life. I turned to everything but Almighty Jesus. By the time my divorce went through, I was a wreck. I had taken all of the skills that I had learned early in life and put them to use. I was now a pawn for satan. I began to do everything that I was big and bad enough to do. I had an excuse. I said that God had forsaken me, but it was me who left God. If it weren't for Him, I probably would be in jail for murder or something

Jan-Dennis Perry

awful. I was a man with no hope. I thought I didn't have a purpose to live. Today I know that no condition is permanent, and I thank God for that.

Chapter Three
The Drug Dealer

After my divorce, I really began to decline. I began to think differently. My self-esteem was in the gutter. I didn't realize it then, but I do now. All of the sins that I had been committing earlier in my life, were now coming back to haunt me I want you to know that God doesn't operate in this realm. Look at Paul he killed Christians, but God turned him around. I guess what I'm trying to tell you is don't let the devil define you buy the acts of your past, but be defined by who you are in God. That wasn't what God had in store for my life or Paul's life.

The devil will use us when we least expect it. As Christians, we have to be careful; the devil and his demons are always lurking around us. They are waiting for an opportunity to use our bodies and minds. I fell right into the devil's trap. I was in a total state of confusion. Confusion is definitely of the devil. My mind wasn't at ease, I didn't have the comfort of Jesus. If I only knew how to pray, fast and glorify His magnificent name, I could have triumphed and been like Hezekiah. I could have praised the Lord no matter what situation was occurring in my life. Paul said we need to be content there within. This means to be content knowing that God is who he said He is, and that no matter what may be going on in our lives know that He is in control.

If I had done this, my book would probably be entirely different. My mind was in torment. I began to increase my participation in the drug trade. Don't let the streets of Huntington fool you they are rough. Then again, street life is rough throughout the country. The projects of any major city are like a country of its own. It is a war, a spiritual war the principalities of good versus principalities of darkness. I don't understand government officials. They say that they want to stop drug activity in the United States, but they don't have many soldiers in the war zone. It's like being in Beirut in some of these projects. You can see everything from gun trade to bartering for clothes. People are selling their bodies, souls and minds in the inner city. I have seen many things in the streets. I have seen hatred, compassion, lust, sex, drugs, violence and many demonic metamorphoses. The inner streets are where the devil likes to lurk most. The devil needs a body to operate out of, and the people who live in the streets are perfect prey. We as church people are going to have to go out into the battle zones. This is where we are needed most. The people in the streets need hope. I think the worse thing I ever saw in the streets as a drug dealer and user is a woman having a baby. This doesn't sound so bad, does it? She was in a dirty old apartment, smoking crack and having a baby. Can you imagine being born under those circumstances?

We have to realize that we are in the last and evil days. The only way out is to accept Jesus Christ as our personal savior. We must repent and turn from our sins. If not, we will perish into the lake of fire, where we will be damned forever. My personal journey through the inner city streets brings me in contact with two individuals whom I mentioned earlier. They are key players at this point in my life. After my divorce, I began to run around with Roger and Kendall. What a crew we were. I continue to pray for them daily. I don't love what we did, but I do love them. God tells me to. We started out like any other low-life thugs. We used to go to the ghetto nightclubs. We would sell dime bags of marijuana. This seemed harmless enough. It was like a popularity contest. We would see who could get the most women, have the most money and dress the best. We didn't even realize that we were poisoning other human beings. I sometimes blame television for the drug trade. It glamorizes drug use and the life of a drug dealer. I like the camaraderie the three of us had; we were like the three musketeers. After selling the marijuana for a while, we thought the money was too slow. This means we had to sell a lot of marijuana to make a good profit. Now remember that at this time I worked at UPS, so I already made good money. As a matter of fact, all three of us worked there. I was trying to fill a void in my life. I think anyone who sells or uses drugs is trying to fill some type of void in his or her life.

We started thinking of the drug game as more than a popularity contest or a way to smoke free weed, or marijuana, by selling drugs to support our own habit. It became a business and big business at that. We moved to the next level, which was cocaine and crack cocaine. Ironic, isn't it? The drug dealer becoming the drug addict. When we moved to the next level, things began to change fast. We were out of our league. When you start selling crack or coke, the clients become more dangerous. I remember when we first started selling crack. We had gone to the dog tracks one afternoon. I never will forget it. I had bet on a dog-named J.D. Alvins. He was a long shot and came in first. I had won $2,600. I wasn't even that excited   I had a pocket full of money when I went. The $2600.00 didn't mean anything to me. We used the money to throw a party that evening. We thought we were big-time hustlers. We rented the union hall. We brought kegs of beer and hot dogs, and we had plenty of crack for sale. Sounds like a nice setup, huh? Let me tell you what happened. We made the news that night. A shoot-out in Huntington, the papers wrote. Several people were injured. That night, a rival crew of ours came from a neighboring town. They came prepared with Uzis and other weapons. They came into the party shooting. I still remember it to this day. There were bullet holes everywhere. I remember some of the cowards in the crowd, men who were supposed to be tough, hiding behind pregnant women. They were using an unborn child as a human shield. One thing about a bullet, it doesn't have eyes. When you're hanging out in the streets, you have to remember there are some people who have no regard for human life. Does this sound like a party to you? This is how the devil operates; he uses us to do his bidding. This is just one of my many early-day drug tales. It was a lucky thing that no one was arrested. We used our fraternity as a front for the party. We didn't even make any money that night; all of our money went to fix the union hall. You would think this would scare us away. It didn't. It made us think that we were now big time. The devil has a way of affecting a person's thinking. I guess that's what it means in the bible when it says the heart is a deceitful thing. Jesus was referring to the human mind, a secular mind. The flesh is truly weak. After the party, we resumed our drug life. It was nothing for us to blow more money than I make in a month today in one afternoon.

Girls, clothes, whiskey, wine and other things that would defile our temple, our bodies. It would make our flesh feel good, but at the same time it was destroying our spirit. We have to overcome the frailties of our human complexities. It is the divine apparatus of the body or flesh to do whatever ever feels good. We have to understand as Christians that this is an obstacle that we face. Life is a war. These are some of the tactics of spiritual warfare. Things may feel good to the flesh but they are terrible for the spirit.

The devil is so deceitful. His war tactics are cunning and skillful. He attacks the spirit with things that make the flesh feel good. I'm here to tell you today that the devil is a liar. He only comes to kill, steal and destroy. I look back and realize how much money and time I wasted. I could have done so many good things with all of that money and time. I could have helped a lot of people. Out of all the things I've done in my life, I hate that I was a drug dealer the most. I can recall several situations when I would control people's actions by their weakness, their habit. I would make men my slaves. I didn't realize I was becoming the devil's slave. I guess you could say at the time I was one of his most faithful servants. When someone is hooked on crack and they are fiendingthey will do anything for another fix or hit of a drug. It was a funny thing when I looked up the word fiend in the dictionary it means an evil spirit, devil, an humanly wicked person or a drug addict, but on the flipside it means one who is excellent at an activity. We have to harness this drug fiend attitude into a positive lifestyle. If somehow we can get people to fiend for Jesus Christ the way that they fiend for drugs and alcohol, we as Christians will be able to take a lot of our young men and women back who are captive to the wiles of the devil. These fiends would knock on my door from morning till night. It was non-stop. I thought my two friends and I were just having a good time. We started getting creative at this point. I would have people work for me. I would buy a little more quantity of coke and cook it up myself. I cooked so much coke one time that I cracked a metal pot. The rock was about the size of a softball. Then I would get someone who was a smoker to sell it on the street for me. They call these people runners. I would play on their weakness. They were often addicts who would sell so they could smoke for free. Does that remind you of my earlier days? I thought I was smoking marijuana and drinking for free. I want you to realize it wasn't for free. I was paying an eternal price with my soul. I thought things were going pretty well. I have to tell you, I don't miss standing out on the corner at 4:00 a.m. I must have been crazy. There isn't anything good out on the streets at that time of the morning. At the time, it seemed kind of exciting. There was something about the thrill of hiding from the police, trying to outsmart them, but I want you to know that you can't outsmart God. He sees all! We went so far to outsmart the cops at one point that my crew and I would place cars throughout Huntington and switch cars all night long. We would switch apartments constantly. We would often find someone who was strung out and give him or her a little bit of coke to let us deal out of his or her home. I told you I would make slaves out of people. I would get a rush from making a deal. I must have been out of my mind; anything could have happened. I saw many a drug dealer held up by someone who was craving drugs. I noticed most of the drug dealing was done at night. I guess somehow we thought God or the police or the people in the neighborhood couldn't see us. They say what is done in the dark will come to the light. This is so true. All the dirt I did in the cover of dark the Lord brought to light. Today, I realize that I'm blessed just to be alive. We had gotten so big that we wouldn't even meet with our connection anymore. We would wire him the money over Western Union. Then he would leave the drugs in a vacant hotel room in Ohio. We wouldn't even see the connection anymore. However, I remember the last time we saw our connection in person. I went to his house in a project off Refugee Road in Columbus, Ohio. I sat down and he kept talking about a million dollars and a freezer full of birds. I didn't really know what he meant. I think he knew this, so he asked me to get a chicken out of the deep freeze. I went to the deep freeze and it was full of cocaine, wrapped in chicken packages. It must have been thirty or forty keys of coke. I couldn't believe it. He then told me that he wanted to show me something. I went back to his bedroom. I was kind of scared; I remember to this day, how fast my heart was racing. He told me to pull back the covers on his bed. There was a million dollars underneath the covers, more money than I saw when I worked at the bank. I told you; although I was a thug I've always had good work ethics. My parents instilled those habits in me. Anyway, when I saw the money it made me nervous. Besides, he had guns everywhere in his apartment. That was the last time I ever met with him in person. We went to wiring the money from there. I was definitely addicted to the power, money and women, and I was fast becoming an alcoholic. I remember ordering a pizza at Donato's Pizza in Columbus from Huntington, then driving three hours to party and eat a pizza. My crew and I would do this as we made a pickup. After doing this for a little while, the connection was busted. The drug flow in Huntington almost came to a complete stop. We were the only ones with any drugs, and this really went to our heads. See, we always put drugs back for a drought. That's when our college education came into play. We were using supply and demand. We would raise the price drastically. I would get people started smoking early in the day. Then I would hide, so that they would fiend. Then I would jack the price of a ten-dollar rock to twenty-five dollars. During this time, things began to really get out of hand. We started partying all the time. I know that I was trying to forget all of my problems. I wish I had only turned to Jesus. I could have easily fallen to my knees, but I didn't. It's a funny thing that when you're doing wrong, you just won't do right. I partied all of that money up and didn't even pay my rent. As things started to get out of hand, I did my normal disappearing act. I left Huntington and went to my parents' house in Clarksburg. This slowed down my drug dealing. There wasn't much demand for crack in Clarksburg. I went back to selling weed. I met a new partner in crime, a girl partner. I won't mention her name because I heard she now has her life together. That girl was a mess. I don't know about now, but back then she could drink with the best of them. She could drink more than a 300-pound truck driver. She could smoke like a Navajo chief. She had good street sense for a little country girl. The devil had set another trap for me. He knew my weakness. He knew I was missing Marie. So he sent me one of his personal concubines, someone to trap my mind. I'm going to jump a little bit ahead. This young lady was vital to my recovery after my car wreck, which I will be going into in great detail in the next chapter. I was working at the time   I had started my career with Agency Rent A Car. I used all those fine marketing techniques that I learned on the streets in business. I was a natural. During this time, I was promoted on my job to an assistant manager at the Fairmont, West Virginia, location. Fairmont is where I picked back up on the serious drug trade. I kept that a secret from everyone. I lived two separate lives. I was a businessman during the day and a street pharmacist at night. I really hooked up with some shady characters. I found that the drugs sold for twice the amount that they had sold in Huntington. These people accepted crumbs for twenty-five dollars in the Clarksburg-Fairmont area. I don't even think my girlfriend knew the extent of my involvement in the drug cartel. She wouldn't have cared anyway. She just wanted to party. Just what I needed, huh? I told you that when the devil sets a trap; he really knows how to do it. I hooked up with a guy I'll call Big Carl. He's in prison today serving a ten-year stint. He was a friend of my Aunt Louisa. That's how we hooked up. When he approached me, he told me he knew my aunt. That was his way into my life. He sort of reminded me of my old crew. He liked to play cards and hustle. Hustling was an art to him. He wasn't someone who used physical violence. He was like me. He would rape you mentally. He would control your mind. Anyway, to make a long story short, we started doing business together. He would take most of the risk. I would front him money and he would give me a profit. This was great; nobody knew. Our final night together is another time Jesus protected my life. I was on my way to see Big Carl and I had noticed that a car was following me all night. I just sort of shrugged it off. I later found out that it was the DEA following me. The DEA is the Drug Enforcement Agency. I don't know what it was, but an inner voice told me to call Big Carl before I went to his hotel room. I went to Kroger's, where I parked to go over to his hotel room. I called his pager on my cell phone as I was walking over to his room. I heard a pager going off, and as I looked up police were everywhere. They had busted him. This was the second friend of mine behind the walls of prison due to drug trafficking. A couple of days later, the DEA came to my work. They wanted to know my involvement with him. I lied and told them I was friends with his grandmother and just came to check on her sometimes. I don't think they bought it, but shortly after that I received a promotion on my job. I was transferred to Asheville, North Carolina, as a general manager. I later became the area manager. I tell you, this drug game worked just like the business world: marketing, supply and demand. I want you parents to realize that there are many things that influence children. One of my own influences was television and rap music. It glamorized this lifestyle, especially the rap music. It told tales of violence, sex and drugs. The people in those videos never have any consequences. It's only a partial reality. I now realize that the devil will use any tool available to him to deceive children, especially music. I know a lot of people don't know that the devil is the minister of music. He knows how to woo his prey. He seduces our fleshly members through music. While I was in Asheville, my drug days ended, except for the weed sales when I would go home to visit my parents. Weed was mighty cheap in the south and I could sell it for a bundle in Clarksburg, although my drug trade really came to an end. My weed smoking and drinking got worse. I really felt alone now. All I had was this female I really didn't like or have anything in common with. No drugs, no Roger, no Kendall, no Big Carl just an empty hole to fill. The devil finally had me where he wanted me. I was so depressed. I stopped paying my bills. I stopped excelling at work. Everything again was falling apart. These were the final days when I sold drugs for the thrill of it. The next time I tell you about selling drugs, I'll be telling you how the devil had set me up all these years to become the addict that I so much despised. I now would be selling the drugs as a necessity to feed my own habit. I do want to take you back to a dramatic event that happened in my life on April 5, 1991. My car wreck was what the devil used as a catalyst to move me to the next level of my destruction . It was the gateway from drug dealer to addict.

Chapter Four
The Car Wreck

April 5, 1991 is a day that I will never forget. It could have been the end. I could have gone to hell for eternity. I could have been burning in a hell's fire pit, hearing the gnashing of teeth. See, I wasn't saved God had to wake me up, or at least get my attention. I was on my way home from Fairmont. I had received a call earlier in the day that someone who had taken some personal property of mine was trying to sell it. I went to confront the person. I made them give me my personal property back, as well as some other stolen possessions that they had acquired. I never got to use my possessions again, as a matter of fact they were strung out all over I-79 (a highway from Clarksburg to Fairmont). I had been drinking with my drinking companion and her family. See, not only did the devil put this young lady in my life who liked to party but her entire family liked to drink and smoke dope. Just what I needed, huh? The devil is a liar. He is only here to steal, kill and destroy, as I will continuously mention. We must not lose sight of his purpose here. The devil really had a trap for my life. After I had gotten my possessions back from the young thug, I got intoxicated with my companion and her family. I was very depressed during this time of my life. I was thinking about my ex-wife, Marie. Remember never look back; this is one of the biggest tricks of the devil. The devil likes to cause confusion, especially in our mind.

I was questioning God; I was wondering why I was facing this in my life. I couldn't handle it, because I didn't have a relationship with Jesus Christ. I blamed God for my wife leaving. I never really faced the issues. I had some doing in her leaving. I wasn't the greatest person in the world, but I thought I had done the best I could do. I believe today that no marriage can make it without Jesus in the center. After drinking heavily with my associate from Fairmont, WV and her family, I began my journey home. All kinds of thoughts were running through my mind. I was in a state of confusion. The devil loves confusion. He can operate in its midst. On the way home, I was reflecting on my marriage. It was the day after Marie's birthday. I was in Clarksburg, not satisfied with my life. I had no peace of mind. I decided that night on the way home that I was going to kill myself. The burden was too much, and I didn't know I could have taken it to the Lord. It was pouring down rain. I could hardly see two feet in front of me. I decided this was it. I shut my eyes and ran the car off the road. I used the car as a weapon of destruction. The car began to flip and head toward the other side of the freeway. My body was ejected from the vehicle and landed on the opposite side of the freeway. My car landed in the middle of the median up against a tree. I remember lying there, unable to move. I felt as if I was urinating on myself, but every time I would feel my groin area, it would be dry. As I lay there half unconscious, my car was leaning against that tree playing a song by Dr. Dre, "Ain't Nothin' but a G Thang." It might as well have been playing,

"It ain't nothin' but a D (devil) thang." See, I was in direct violation of the laws of God. I was trying to take my own life. I would have spent eternity in hell. Thank God, He had other plans for me. God sent an angel from heaven. A truck driver was coming down the road. He saw the accident. He saw me lying there in the middle of the road. He pulled his truck in the middle of the freeway to block all traffic. I was lying in the middle of the freeway, facing oncoming cars. To this day, I have tried to thank the truck driver, but no one could ever locate him. I believe he is back in heaven. I don't think the driver was of this earth. He was one of God's angels sent to protect me. God has a plan for my life. Something great. I have heard that Jesus used a lot of people to stand in the gap for me that night. There were some spectacular EMTs on duty that night, as well as a surgeon named Dr. Patrick Galey. I don't remember much at this point.

The next thing I remember is waking up in the hospital. I was very weak and groggy. It seemed like a bad nightmare. I looked down on my body and saw this contraption. It looked like something out of a science fiction movie. It went around my entire waist. It had two steel poles that went right through my waist. It had a big metal bar extending from each pole. If you have ever seen the halos that people wear when they fracture their necks, this is what I had on my waist, except it went clear through my side. It screwed in like a big wood screw. I had one bag on my right side that was full of urine and another on my left full of blood. My arm was bandaged pretty heavily. I couldn't talk. I had a tube in my throat helping me to breathe. I remember looking up and seeing my mom. I was breaking her heart. She has always been there for me a little over-protective at times, but I think I have made her that way. She had my clothes in her hand. They were torn to shreds. My dad was right there.

This was only the second time in my life that I had ever seen him cry. The first was when they diagnosed my mom with melanoma cancer stage four. They only gave her six months to live. I remember he reacted the same way in both situations. He prayed. Back then I didn't know what he knew, but I do now. He was having prayer with the Lord. He had a relationship with the most high. My dad truly had favor. He can stand in the gap for me any day. I overheard my dad praying that if he had any favor with God to spare my life. I remember he said the same prayer over my mother. We are both alive and well today. My injuries consisted of a shattered pelvis, busted bladder, compound fracture of the arm and broken spirit.

I lay there in the United Hospital Center thinking that I would never walk again. My problems had quadrupled overnight. I decided that I wanted to live after all. Just think, had I died, I wouldn't have found Jesus, my beloved wife Nicole and my two precious children, Ayshia and Robert. I had a Vietnamese doctor who gave me some inspiration. He didn't know he was giving it to me, but he did. The doctor thought I was asleep, but I wasn't. He was telling the nurse that he had seen my type of injuries before in Vietnam. He told her I was spoiled goods, I would never be the same and I was going to sour. That's when I had a conversation with God. I asked Him to let me live and walk again.

The doctor was right I never was quite the same, but I did recover health-wise. The doctor didn't know that the doctor of all doctors, the Mighty Counselor Jireh the Provider, could restore me. God had and has a purpose for my life. He put some incredible people in position to help restore me physically. I remember my dad searching for the best medical attention for me. He found Dr. Dana C. Mears, the inventor of pelvic surgery. He was a doctor who specialized in pelvic injuries. My family had me moved to Pittsburgh, Pennsylvania, where I met Dr. Mears. He said he could put my pelvis back together and I would walk again. Praise God, I have to just take a moment out to praise Him, because He has been so good to me. I had some struggles. I had to relearn how to walk. We take so many things for granted. I actually had my ability to walk taken away for about six months. During the first few months of rehabilitation, the pain was intolerable. This is where my fire for narcotics was lit. The doctors hooked me up with a morphine pump. I couldn't handle this. One night after an injection with morphine, I began to break out in cold sweats. I itched all over; I also began to hallucinate . I saw clowns and goblins after me. I didn't realize it then but the devil and his demons were trying to destroy my mind. I believe that they thought they had me when I tried to kill myself on I-79. They wanted my soul badly I had always been a good soldier for them. If I had succeeded in killing myself, the devil would have had me for eternity. God had different plans; He himself came down and wrapped His arms around me. Jesus put a hedge of protection around me. The morphine scared me; I was allergic. The doctors then hooked me up to a Demerol pump. This is a machine for people experiencing extreme pain. It is directly hooked up to your veins, and you can inject yourself with the narcotic at a push of a button. The devil has many vessels he can use. Whoever dreamed that I had the gene of addiction in my body? I had been around cocaine for some time. I could have had as much as I would have liked. I never had tried it. The devil now had an opportunity to use my weakness against me. Remember, the devil has no real power to do us harm unless we give him a vessel to use, and he can't dwell where the Holy Spirit lives. When that Demerol flowed through my veins, all my worries and pain went away, at least for a little while. I could not only escape my excruciating pain but my emotional pain. To this day, I think the devil had been setting me up for the crossroads of my life. I honestly know that Jesus has great plans for me today. If not, the devil wouldn't have tried so hard to steal, kill and destroy my soul, body and mind. I realize today that the devil was after my mind. After a while, I began to feel myself becoming dependent on the Demerol. The doctor and I began to notice. I started to wean myself off the Demerol. I then moved to Percoset painkillers. These didn't make me forget anything. They just made the pain subside for a little bit.

While I was working on walking, I had a lot of time to think. I thought about my life. It was awful, no peace of mind. The devil was still on the attack. I hadn't talked to my ex-wife in months. She called me as I lay there in the bed. She didn't say a kind word; she just wanted to know if I was alive. I must have really hurt her, because she was cold-hearted toward me. Of course, I never made amends with her. I would pray, but it seemed like my prayers were blocked. I had never repented and wasn't willing to change. I was still trying to take my life into my own hands. I didn't want to give up control of my life. I had said to myself when I get out of the hospital, I'm going to make a change and quit drinking and smoking weed. I did this for about nine months. Of course, the first three to six months were easy. I couldn't function on my own. I depended on my family to feed me, cloth me and even help me use the bathroom. I was like an infant. After I got out of the hospital, I still had a long way to recovery. I was on crutches. I couldn't walk on my own. I went through rehab at the United Hospital Center . Dr. Pat Galey, the surgeon who first put me back together, has a wife who helped me with my physical therapy. She pushed me to walk again. She was another one of God's angels who helped restore me physically. I had some angels all this time looking out for me. I remember the pastor who baptized me. He would come around and take me to physical therapy when my parents were unable. Jesus has a way of putting people into positions to help you. has Although he had some issues of his own, he was always there for me. Should I down him for his own issues? I think not. I should love him because a sinner is just a saint who fell down. The bible says a just man falleth seven times, and riseth up again: but the wicked shall fall into mischief. I know throughout my story you've heard me mention the devil's trap. I need you to realize that the warfare is in your mind. The devil is trying to steal your mind. He wants you to give up, but I'm here to tell you if life begins to be too much cling to your rope, tie a knot and hold on, your help is on the wayThe Lord had a plan for me. I didn't know it back then, but I know now that if it weren't for my personal savior Jesus Christ, I would be a lost sheep, and there is nothing worse than to be lost and no one looking for you.

My friends, or so-called friends, never came around. They never so much as offered me a glass of water. I want some of the younger folks who think it is cool to be a gangster to remember this portion of the book. It is true; when you get down those people you caused mischief with won't be there for you. They will only criticize and ridicule your poor decision-making. Christian folks had prayer lines going on for me all over the state of West Virginia. It wasn't until I began to walk again and function on my own that my so-called friends came around. I hadn't put anything into my temple in quite a while. The devil had found a vessel to use. He needed something to draw me back into the life of corruption. A friend of mine came to pick me up and was supposed to cheer me up, but I believe the enemy, which is the devil, sent him to get me back on the side of the devil. The devil used one of his oldest traps for me. Then again, why get something new when you know what works? As we went out, we ran into some girls we had never seen before. I had a gift with the ladies. I began to talk to them, and the next thing I knew, we were over at their house drinking beer and committing fornication. The devil had a trap set. I realize that he uses people. Why else would two attractive young ladies be interested in us? I was darn near crippled at the time. These girls were the devil's concubines. They were on one of his missions. I had let the devil win another battle, but he didn't win the war. I do have to say that. I don't want anyone to read this book at any time and believe he won. He didn't. He's a liar. Remember, I hadn't drunk or used drugs in about six months during this time. You wouldn't believe how I started right where I left off. My tolerance for alcohol was the same, if not more. I went into a stage of guilt. I had promised myself that I wouldn't drink anymore. I knew it was trouble, but I wasn't strong enough to fight against the devil without the blood of Jesus. I was at a crossroads in my life. At this stage, my life could have been entirely different. I could have chosen Jesus then and saved myself a lot of hurt and pain instead of taking the road that seemed the easiest, which is another trick of the devil. I took the broad road of life. It almost killed me. I missed many of my blessings on this road. Instead, it took me on the road of addiction.

Chapter Five
The Drug Addict

This chapter is the hardest of all the chapters to write about. It is where the devil nearly destroyed my life. Thank God for His divine wisdom and intervention. If it were not for God's grace and mercy, I would have surely perished. This is a chapter of many dedications, the prayers of the righteous avail much in the kingdom of heaven. A lot of people stood in the gap for me when I was unable to help or pray for myself. I had a lot of prayer warriors who kept the principalities of darkness from taking my soul. My soul now belongs to the King, who is King Jesus. Even with all the miraculous works that Jesus had been doing in my life, I still hadn't turned my will and life over to His care. I was looking in all the wrong places for comfort. I didn't realize that Jesus had sent a comforter a long time ago. The Holy Spirit was always there to teach and comfort me, but I wouldn't give it a clean temple in which to dwell. At this time in my life, I should have seen God's divine providence over me; God had spared me from going to prison for dealing drugs. He had also spared me from the violence that came with that lifestyle. I had even been given a modern-day miracle; the Lord had spared my life in a horrible car accident. As a matter of fact, Christ healed me when the doctors told me that I would never be able to walk again. I want you to know that I am a living testimony; today, I not only walk but also play a pretty mean game of basketball. Even seeing all God's healings and divine providence, I still wouldn't take my burdens to the Lord. I turned instead to worldly ways. I tried to drown my sorrows in a liquor bottle or by smoking marijuana. I think that I had always been an alcoholic and an addict but was never willing to see the writing on the wall. Who wants to believe he has a drug or alcohol problem? Surely not me, or anyone else that I know would want to have that stigma of being an alcoholic or drug addict. I did not want to be viewed as someone with a problem of that nature. I wanted to be viewed as "normal", but by whose standards, we all must ask ourselves-, whose standards are we living by? Is it the standards of the world or the standards of Christ Jesus who died for the remission of our sins..

When I look at things on a more spiritual level, I believe I had a generational curse that had to be broken in my family. My grandfathers from my mother's and father's sides of the family both had died from alcoholism, and there were uncles, aunts and others who were unwilling to admit the possibility of substance abuse problems. It was a hush-hush topic in my family. I was not able to see that I was already in a spiritual warfare; I began to drink and drug more heavily. My real troubles with drugs started one weekend in May 1993. I was a district manager for Agency Rent A Car. I had gone home to Huntington to be with my sister Erica. She had won a social studies fair competition. I went home to hear terrible tales about my ex-wife. See, the devil had a trap set for me. I went to one of my friends' homes in Huntington and began to hear all kinds of things about my ex-wife and our marriage that I didn't know. This is where I found out that she was with child, meaning that she was pregnant. I couldn't emotionally handle this; it was something at this time I definitely did not want to hear. I wasn't happy with my life; I was distraught about all that was going on. How did we get to this point where someone is telling me that the person I loved so dearly is having someone else's child? This incident brought me to a major crossroads in my life. My friends, or so-called friends, told me that they had something that could make me forget all of my troubles. It was new to me, but this demon has walked the streets of the United States for years. It was crack cocaine. The mention of its name sickens me. Today, I call it the devil's rock. It was a direct link right to the pits of hell. It was true that it made me forget all of my problems. It was like an aphrodisiac at first. I will never forget the first hit off the crack pipe. It made me feel that everything was all right. I was in a state of mind that I will never forget. The building could have been burning down around me and I would have sat there without flinching. The devil led me to believe that this was my newest and dearest friend. It was an escape an escape from reality, but very short-lived. The problem with the drug was that there were never enough drugs, nor would there ever be enough drugs, to escape all of life's difficulties unless you reached the final high that took you to death. If you don't remember anything else in this book, remember that drugs and alcohol are substances that alter your mood and mind physical and emotional effects that you have no control over. The warfare of life is in your mind. The struggle is in your mind. The devil's goal is to steal your mind. God has not given you the spirit of fear but of power, of love and of a sound mind. It is with the mind that we serve the Lord. As an addict I have suffered many trials, many battles of the mind. It was hard for me to admit such a curse plagued me, but I wasn't willing to allow it to overcome me. It didn't matter how many battles I had to lose, I was not going to succumb to the death grip of the devil. I can't describe to you in words the feeling of being an addict, only those who have endured this trial knows of what I speak of. It is beyond human comprehension. This is why every addict needs the divine intervention of God to deliver you from this that has afflicted you. For you that are addicts, and I speak of addiction of any kind, know that God is the answer. He will not only deliver you, but also restore you completely. Remember, when tempted pray without ceasing. Prayer changes things, I am a witness, and you can be one as well, as to the mercy of God.

Chapter Six
The Warfare

I realize today that drug addiction is a war that is declared on the mind by the devil. The bible tells me that the true battle is in the mind. In Romans 7:25, scripture tells me it is with the mind that I myself serve the law of God, but with the flesh the law of sin.

It is the flesh that allowed the devil to use all of my weaknesses against me. The devil declared war on my mind one more time. This is how the devil causes a relapse in an addict's life. I know that a lot of science and medical information gives us a lot of great help, such as twelve-step programs, but the truth of the matter is that addiction is a struggle of the mind. It's a lack of rest in the mind. Have you ever gone to bed and woken up tired? Have you ever woken up and the bed was a mess, as if you were in a struggle all night long? I have woken up in a puddle of sweat, like I wrestled with the devil all night long. As a matter of fact, for several years of my life prior to accepting Jesus Christ as my personal savior, I had the same recurring nightmare night after night. The devil was chasing me through the streets torturing me. I bet for several years I never got any rest. Now that I serve the Lord with my mind, body and soul, I sleep like a baby.

Addiction and relapse are a terrible torment of the mind. The bible clearly states that when we allow sin back into our lives, the torment gets worse. I think this is what clinical practitioners mean when they say that drugs and alcohol have a natural progression even when we aren't using drugs and alcohol. This is why twelve-step programs are a way of life. It is a change. It's a form of repentance, meaning turning away from one's evil and wicked ways. It not only means abstaining from drugs and alcohol but turning from all sin. I know firsthand how the devil operates in warfare. He uses one sin as an opening to gain entrance back into our lives. Scripture tells us in Luke that when a strong man armed keepeth his palace, his goods are in peace, but when a stronger than he shall come upon him, and overcome him, he "taketh from him all his armour wherein he trusted, and divideth his spoils". When we allow sin to overcome us and destroy our armour, it's a very dangerous state; we become vulnerable to relapsing and possibly death. As a matter of fact, one of the spiritual principles of warfare occurs when we allow sin back into our lives. In Luke 11:26, scripture says "that he, the devil, go and taketh to him seven other spirits more wicked than himself". Can you imagine the devil bringing back spirits more wicked than himself? Then they enter in and dwell there, and your last state is far worse than your first. (This is a stage of progression in today's medical terminology.) I know firsthand that this is a reality of spiritual warfare. I experienced this firsthand. I allowed sin to creep into my life and things were worse than they had ever been. I allowed sin to enter into my life and hid it from all those close to me but not from God. God is omnipotent; He knows everything. I then allowed the devil to fester, that which was hidden within me. This is where the heart of my battle took place. I need you to know that this is a serious situation. It is a matter of life and death. The devil is here to kill you. He is here to destroy your mind.

My relapse occurred way before I picked up a drink or drug. The attack was on my spiritual character months before I used. It was prophesized to me that the devil had come back with not only several unclean spirits, but also seven of his generals. They had come to kill and destroy me. I realize today that it wasn't me, really, they were trying to destroy, but my ministry. The devil doesn't care about Jan-Dennis Perry but he cares about the numbers that might be won over to Christ through my ministry.

It was during this stage of my life that I realized that this life that we live today is not as it seems. We are in a war. We are in a battle of good and evil. The bible tells me that we wrestle not against flesh and blood but against principalities, powers, rulers of darkness of this world, spiritual wickedness in high places. How fitting for my major conflict to take place in the nation's capital, Washington, D.C. or, as I call it, Sodom and Gomorrah. My experience took on a lot of supernatural characteristics. If it weren't for the intercessory prayer of Jesus Christ himself, I would have lost my mind. He used a lot of extraordinary people to show me His mercy and grace. I could go on to tell you a lot of drug tales, but I won't give the devil any glory or honor in this book. I will highlight some things for you though. When I allowed the devil back into my life through some cracks that I had in my armour, he came back more fierce than ever. The devil and his generals were trying to destroy my mind and everything that I believed in. I believe they knew this was the final battle in my life over drug and alcohol addiction. I spent thousands and thousands of dollars trying to ease my mind, trying to forget my problems. The real battle laid dormant waiting on an opportunity to manifest itself and overtake me. The grips of addiction took me to new heights. I was using for days at a time, with no rest or sleep. It was supernatural. I was able to stay up for four or five days without any sleep, without anything to eat or drink, without taking a bath for days on end. One of the lowest moments that I can remember is being out of money driving a an expensive luxury car, hungry from not eating or drinking in days, and proudly pulling up to a soup line to get something to eat. Remember, I had told you that the devil would bring back several more unclean spirits. He definitely did in my case. I had become a thief, a liar and a terrible husband and father, but most of all I had become a fallen Christian. This is one of the things that the devil used the most against me in this warfare. I had simply made some mistakes that I could have corrected easily by seeking the Lord. All I had to do was ask for forgiveness. The devil used this against me in my mind. He kept telling me things such as I would never be a preacher again who would respect a preacher who went off and had a drink? He used this to gain entry so that he could put fear in my mind and cause me to use drugs, which he knew was a for-sure weakness of mine. I need all of you reading this book to know that the devil uses people, places and things to cause havoc in our lives. This is one of the principles of a recovering addict. We must change all people, places and things. This means we need to change our whole lifestyle. To me, it means live a holy and righteous life. Remember, salvation is instantaneous but sanctification is a process. So, easy does it. Remember, you didn't become an addict overnight, so do things in moderation.

I have given you just a few examples of the horrible nightmare when I allowed the devil entry into my life. Let me give you some of the great examples of the favor that God had on my life. I remember one day riding around the streets of D.C. and feeling like the Holy Ghost was following me around. As a matter of fact, I thought I was going crazy that day. I was riding around with a shady fellow and a couple of his friends. I began to speak in tongues riding around. I thought for sure that I had lost my mind. I now realize that God was intervening on my behalf. I got to my destination, which was a hotel room in a rough section of southeast D.C., the murder capital of the world. I hadn't taken a shower or slept in a few days. I had about a quarter ounce of cocaine in my possession. I went to take a shower. Remember, I had told you that I felt like the Holy Ghost had been following me all day. Well, He had. He couldn't dwell within me because my temple was defiled, but God had a purpose in my life. He had started a good work within me a few years back and He promises that He will finish those things till the end. When I got out of the shower, I felt odd. I sat down in a chair in this hotel room and felt very uncomfortable. I can't really explain it, but something extraordinary happened. I jumped up out of the chair, dropped all of my cocaine, crack stem and cigarettes and began to tell the people in the room that I was a minister and that ministers do not act like I was acting. I ran out of the room crying profusely. I called my wife and told her that God had told me that He would deliver me as long as I told the truth to anyone I had stolen from or lied to. I could have ended my nightmare right then, but I let the devil put ideas into my head. He was telling me things like I would lose my job, my freedom   nobody would understand, so just tell some half-truths. He even used my family to validate some of those feelings. We all looked at things in the flesh

49

when it came to things dealing with man. I am a living witness that God is not slack concerning His promises. If God speaks something to you, you don't have anything to worry about unless you are disobedient. In Isaiah 1:19, Jesus says "if ye be willing and obedient, ye shall eat the good of the land, but if ye refuse and rebel, ye shall be devoured with the sword: for the mouth of the Lord hath spoken". When I didn't obey God, needless to say I was devoured. Even with all this, God still had mercy on me. I had all kinds of things happen to me in between, but God was there protecting His lost sheep when I couldn't defend myself. There are two examples that can't be explained by anything natural, just by God's favor. I was once pulled over by the Virginia state police at about 4:30 a.m. I was doing about 85 mph in a 55 mph zone. I hadn't slept in a couple of days and had just drunk a pint of pure moonshine. I somehow passed the DUI test. My blood alcohol level was .07 and the legal limit was .08. The funny thing is that right before I was pulled over, I had put a whole thing of Listerine breath strips in my mouth. Was this a coincidence? I think not. It was God's grace. Another incident: I ran a red light coming out of a shady area of town and crossed over three lanes right in front of a policeman. He put on his lights and pulled up beside me and told me to be careful. God has control over everything. It was through His grace and mercy that I didn't kill myself or anyone else. You see, He will even intervene on our behalf when we are out of His will. One of the greatest things that I have learned through this warfare is to keep God's word in my heart. To know His word and to live his word, is very important. To know it is the truth and to have faith. The Bible says "faith is the substance of things hoped for and the evidence of things not seen".

Who am I to challenge the word of God? When I didn't have faith and when I wasn't listening to God speak to my heart, it went from bad to worse. But can you imagine being drawn into this warfare when you don't even have an addiction problem?

Chapter Seven
Through Her Eyes

How did I get myself into this mess? I have asked myself too. I cannot believe the turn of events in my life. There has to be a purpose, a meaning to the madness. Lord God, why me? I found myself asking these types of questions. Let me begin with what a typical episode would be like for me. It takes you by surprise each time, because you do not want to believe that your loved one has fallen again to this same demon. Then for me the anger sets in. It angers me because I do not have a substance abuse problem; I have never even smoked a "joint". So why am I going through this? You may ask me the same thing. Well, I had made a vow before God to honor, love and cherish "in sickness and in health", so that is what I chose to do. Yes, for all of those who do not believe drug addiction is a sickness, you must rethink that concept and research the matter. I was one of the biggest skeptics concerning the fact that drug addiction was a disease. I felt that you could stop when you wanted to, if you wanted to, but in reality these individuals do not have that luxury.

So, once you get over the initial shock, you go into a protection mode. When I say protection mode, I must explain what I am speaking of. You can't let anyone know this secret. It has to be hidden and kept amongst the immediate family   the addict, his wife and possibly his parents. You must carry on as if everything is okay. You begin to block all means of the addict obtaining any money or valuables. You cut off debit cards, freeze accounts, whatever is necessary not to feed the addiction with your money or the addict's, for that matter. Can you imagine all that you have worked for and saved is spent in a few days' time? It will send the sanest person into a rage. This drug not only milks you dry financially, but emotionally and physically, and it attempts to spiritually destroy you. Yes, you, the one who does not have a drug problem. You attempt to protect the addict's job, the cars, the house and even the addict's reputation, but it is all fair game since the addict has invited the devil into your life.

During this warfare, I had many restless and sleepless nights wondering if he was dead or alive. I was unable to eat and my health had begun to deteriorate, but I had to maintain this "normal" life. I remember praying to God on his behalf for deliverance in his life. I found myself in constant prayer and conversation with God. I was interceding on his behalf. I was praying because I loved him, and I knew he could not pray for himself. I was angry, but yet compassionate. I wanted God to spare him still another time. He has a work to finish and this is not the person I married and loved.

One day during this incident, during this warfare, which happened to be my birthday, was a turning point for me. I had never felt so betrayed in my life. I had seen him that morning and had told him that I didn't want any chaos on this particular day. I did not want this day plagued with any thoughts of drugs or the problems that come with drugs. He did not even know it was my birthday. Now this is someone who has always done something special or brought me something meaningful for this day, and he didn't even know it was my birthday. I was dumbfounded, almost in a state a shock. He began to plead for money and act a little irrational. I refused and told him to leave. I was furious at the state he had fallen to. Lord God, what is happening? Finally, after much persistence I gave in and gave him fifteen dollars with the condition that he leave town. Of course, that was a vain promise, and I knew that. I just wanted this moment to be over so that I could go and try to have an unrealistically "normal" day.

In the midst of all of this, I too had fallen to the snares of the devil. I had allowed sin to come into my life and work to destroy my marriage. I was starting to give up. I wasn't getting the answers I needed quickly enough from the Lord, and I too fell into despair. The devil will use and do anything to attack and discredit the works of the Lord. I wanted so much for everything to be okay, but I was tired and I didn't have much fight left in me. That is when the Lord took over; see, the Lord tells me that His grace is sufficient, for His strength takes over in my weakness. I gained some things through the trials of my faith. I realize today that faith is much more precious than gold. I know that God, whom I have not yet seen, loves me unconditionally. I come to the conclusion today that this walk with my husband is a battle, that we were in a war together and I am truly a good soldier in this warfare. The bible tells me in 2 Timothy 2:3 that I must endure hardness as a good soldier for Jesus Christ.

At my weakest moment, I let go and let God. I, like my husband, began to seek the Lord and He heard me and delivered us from all our fears. When you find yourself in a situation such as mine, remember to trust in the Lord and that a wise woman buildeth her house, but the foolish plucketh it down with her hands. I could have easily used my trials and tribulations as an excuse to let our marriage be destroyed, but I realized that it was more than just my husband and I, but a ministry as well, that would have perished.

Chapter Eight
Jails, Institutions and Death

Through all of my trials and tribulations, the devil tried to steal a lot of blessings that were predestined for my life. I have to tell you everything that he meant for bad, my Lord and savior made positive and good. It makes me reflect on God's word where He tells us that the devil comes to steal, kill and destroy, but Jesus comes so that we might have life and have it more abundantly. This will be a rather short chapter because the devil has no victory in my life. I have to forewarn anyone who wants to enter into the life of drugs and alcohol that it only ends in three categories: jails, institutions and death. I have to say jail is an inhumane place. Of course, man wants us to believe that jails are a place for rehabilitation. As we look at the root of the word penitence, which is the root word for penitentiary, it means to pay for or a consequence of our actions. There isn't anything in the word that would reference rehabilitation. I believe that we should definitely pay for our crimes, but we should be allowed to do so and then live a productive life. How do we do this? First of all, there has to be some type of reform or training in these institutions. The only thing I ever learned from one of these places is how to become a better criminal or a more advanced drug user. Jails are where I learned my most devious behavior. I believe that President Bush is on the right track when he talks about faith-based community programs. These programs allow churches to nurture people and families who went through a crisis back to being productive members of society. The only thing is that we have to be careful not to worry so much about politics and social reform that we don't give God the credit.

As for institutions, I spent some time in mental institutions during my warfare. I do appreciate the assistance that I have received from drug rehabilitation centers, but they will never be totally effective until they admit that this is a spiritual warfare. It is an attack on the very fiber of mankind. I believe that the institutions were birthed as a sanctuary by Christians such as Bill Wilson, but man and his warped thinking have taken the concept of God out of the concept of the twelve-step program. Here are the twelve steps that I use, which are all about God being the center of my recovery.

Twelve Spiritual Steps of Warfare Recovery

1. WE ADMITTED THAT WE HAD BECOME POWERLESS OVER ALCOHOL OR THE ALCOHOLIC (THE SUBSTANCE WE HAD ABUSED OR THE SUBSTANCE ABUSER) AND THAT OUR LIVES WERE UNMANAGEABLE.
2. WE CAME TO BELIEVE THAT THROUGH JESUS CHRIST WE COULD BE RESTORED TO A RIGHT RELATIONSHIP WITH GOD THE FATHER AND SUBSEQUENT SANITY AND STABILITY IN OUR LIVES.

3. WE MADE THE DECISION TO TURN FROM THE THINGS OF THE PAST AND INVITE JESUS TO BE THE LORD AND MANAGER OF OUR LIVES.

4. WE MADE A SEARCHING AND FEARLESS MORAL INVENTORY OF OURSELVES.

5. WE ADMITTED TO GOD, OURSELVES AND ANOTHER HUMAN BEING THE EXACT NATURE OF OUR WRONGS.

6. WE'RE ENTIRELY READY TO HAVE GOD REMOVE ALL OF OUR CHARACTER DEFECTS.

7. WE HUMBLY ASKED GOD TO REMOVE OUR SHORTCOMINGS AND TO FORGIVE US   BELIEVING GOD CAN REMOVE THEM AND RECEIVING HIS FORGIVENESS.

8. WE MADE A LIST OF ALL THE PEOPLE WE HAD HARMED AND BECAME WILLING TO MAKE AMENDS TO THEM ALL.

9. WE MADE DIRECT AMENDS TO SUCH PEOPLE, WHEREVER POSSIBLE, EXCEPT WHEN TO DO SO WOULD INJURE THEM OR OTHERS.

10. WE CONTINUED TO TAKE PERSONAL INVENTORY AND WHEN WE WERE WRONG, PROMPTLY ADMITTED IT.

11. WE SOUGHT THROUGH PRAYER AND MEDITATION ON GOD'S WORD TO INCREASE OUR FELLOWSHIP WITH HIM, PRAYING CONTINUALLY FOR THE KNOWLEDGE OF HIS WILL FOR US AND THE POWER OF *HIS* MIGHT TO ACCOMPLISH IT.

12. HAVING BEEN SPIRITUALLY RESTORED AND SET FREE FROM "THE SIN WHICH DOES EASILY BESET US", WE ATTEMPTED TO SHARE THIS FREEDOM AND THE *ONE* WHO HAS FREED US WITH THOSE WHO STILL SUFFER AND PRACTICE THE LORD'S PRINCIPLES IN ALL OUR AFFAIRS.

If we don't start living a holy and righteous life, we will surely meet a gruesome death. It is true that as addicts we face many deaths, such as relationships, jobs, family ties, miss our children grew up, but the most awful death would be to die in the grips of addiction, and be unsaved, this would mean that we would live life in eternal damnation. The bible tells me that our bodies would surely die, but our souls would burn in the lake of fire forever and ever. The bible tells us in the book of Matthew that when we are cut off from Christ, the children of the kingdom will be cast down into outer darkness; there will be weeping and the gnashing of teeth. This makes me realize that the struggle I am enduring during this warfare is nothing compared to the suffering and pain that I would endure in hell. I do realize that the world and the devil would love for us to think that death, that would be the easy way out. I often would hear people say that they would rather die than go through all of the hell that comes from drug addiction, but I would rather suffer and have one more chance to repent and live a good live. The bible says that he that endures to the end shall be saved.

Chapter Nine
The Restoration

I thank the Lord for the restoration of my mind, soul, body, family, marriage, job, career and ministry, and for His favor. Yes, it is true the devil did steal my joy for a season, but thank goodness for God's grace and mercy, for His love for many others and me, the devil has desired to sift as wheat. Just know that if we seek God's guidance and His will, He can restore you and me. It makes me think of David when he had gone out of God's realm, but when he had asked God what to do, God had told David to pursue after his enemy and that he would surely recover all without fail. I remember my restoration as if it were yesterday. I didn't have any fancy prayer; I didn't have time to go into any ceremonial routine. I just began to holler out Lord help me at that very moment I was able to touch the hem of his garment and be made whole. A modern-day miracle! A restoration of my mind! The restoration of my family! Since that time, I have gone on to seek the Lord with all my heart and soul. His word is no longer words I spew from my mouth, but it is indwelled within my very being. It is now buried in my heart and the deepest parts of my soul. See, I called on the

Lord and He heard me and delivered me from all my fears. He restored my ministry. He made the love my wife has for me stronger than it has ever been. Her love and compassion truly endured to the end. He made me the father that He wanted me to be all along. I'm not bragging, just giving God all the glory and praise. I thank God for all my material things, such as a brand new home, a Jaguar, nice clothes and an exalted career, but most of all I thank God for the worship He has implanted in my being. I now know the difference between praise and worship. If I had not been restored with the gifts of this world, I would still worship my God. I am now content when I have and content when I have not. My only desire is to be found in the vineyard doing the work and the will of my Lord and Savior Jesus Christ.

Without my life's trials , I wouldn't have the testimony that I have today. I love the Lord with all my heart and soul. I thank God for His holy word, which I stand on today. The Lord has taken me to the 51st Psalm the 12th and 13th verses. He has restored unto me the joy of my salvation and upheld me with a free spirit. Now I am able to do the work of the Lord and teach transgressors His way, and sinners shall be converted. Now I am a true soldier in the army of the Lord. The devil may have won a couple of battles, but Jesus has won the war. It is with this that I was made a new creature in Christ. Scripture tells me that I am a new creature, old things have been passed away, all things are made new and all things in my life are now of God. There is no more secret sin; God has reconciled Himself to me. He has given to me the ministry of reconciliation, and with this I pass on to you some of the gifts that God has birthed within me. I share with you some of the teaching and preaching God has anointed in my spirit through several of my sermons. I want to arm you for battle with God's word, do not only read them, but hide them in your heart. There will be a time that you will need these teaching when in a battle.

Chapter Ten
Sermons of Inspiration
WEAPONS OF WARFARE
HOW DID I GET MYSELF INTO THIS MESS?

SCRIPTURES: JUDGES 13 THROUGH THE 16TH CHAPTERS.

HAVE YOU EVER BEEN IN A MESS? WE ARE GOING TO TAKE A LOOK AT A MAN WHO SURELY ASKED HIMSELF THAT QUESTION. THE MAN'S NAME IS SAMSON. SAMSON WAS ONE OF THE MOST OUTSTANDING JUDGES OF BIBLICAL TIMES. HE WAS THE JUDGE AND RULER OF ISRAEL FOR TWENTY YEARS. SAMSON HAD AN OPPORTUNITY MORE SO THAN ANY OTHER MAN TO DO THE WORK OF THE LORD. SAMSON WAS A UNIQUE AND HAD TREMENDOUS POTENTIAL. HE WASN'T UNIQUE BECAUSE OF HIS PHYSICAL STRENGTH, BUT BECAUSE OF HIS SPIRITUAL STRENGTH. EVERYTHING ABOUT SAMSON'S LIFE WAS SET FOR A BRILLIANT CAREER AND FUTURE.

ALTHOUGH SAMSON HAD A GREAT FOUNDATION FOR SUCCESS HE STILL MANAGED TO FALL INTO SOME OF LIFE'S TRAPS. SAMSON PROBABLY ASKED THE QUESTION, HOW DID I GET MYSELF IN THIS MESS? WHEN YOU HEAR SAMSON'S NAME

YOUR IMMEDIATELY THINK OF A MAN WITH SUPER STRENGTH AND STAMINA. YOU MIGHT EVEN THINK OF HIM AS A MODERN DAY SUPERMAN, BUT I'M HERE TO TELL YOU THAT IF YOUR SPIRITUAL STRENGTH ISN'T AS STRONG AS YOUR NATURAL STRENGTH YOU ARE SET FOR FAILURE.

SAMSON'S STRENGTH WAS BASED ON HIS SPIRITUAL VALUES, BECAUSE OF HIS NASSERITE VOWS. HE WAS INSTILLED FROM THE VERY BEGINNING WITH THREE SIGNIFICANT VOWS:

1. HE WAS NOT TO TOUCH STRONG DRINK OR USE GRAPES IN ANY FORM. (HE WAS TO FIND HIS JOY IN THE LORD.) HE WAS TO HAVE THE FRUITS OF THE SPIRIT.
2. HE WAS NO TO CUT HIS HAIR. (1 CORINTHIAN 11:14)
3. HE WAS NOT TO GO NEAR A DEAD BODY.

ALL THREE OF THESE ARE PERTINENT RULES THAT WERE SYMBOLS OF OBEDIENCE TO GOD. TODAY WE HAVE THE NEW TESTAMENT AS A GUIDELINE FOR HOLY LIVING. RULES WILL DETERMINE OUR SUCCESS IN LIFE. WHEN WE DO THE RIGHT THING, THE RIGHT THINGS WILL COME OUR WAY. GOD DOESN'T WANT US TO PUT ANYTHING BEFORE HIM. WE HAVE LOST SIGHT OF THIS TODAY. WE AS CHRISTIANS PUT SO MANY THINGS BEFORE OUR LORD AND SAVIOR JESUS CHRIST. WE HAVE ALL KINDS OF EXCUSES ABOUT BEING OBEDIENT TO THE WILL OF GOD. WE COMPLAIN ABOUT OUR CHRISTIAN LEADERS AND THOSE WITH RULE AND AUTHORITY OVER US. WE HAVE A LOT OF EXCUSES WHEN IT COMES TO SERVING GOD AND DOING WHAT IS RIGHT. AS YOU READ ON YOU MIGHT FIND THE MESSAGE A LITTLE TIGHT, BUT I GUARANTEE YOU THAT THE MESSAGE WILL BE RIGHT. IT WILL HELP YOU TO UNDERSTAND HOW WE OFTEN GET IN THE MESSES THAT WE DO WHEN TRAVELING THROUGH LIFE'S JOURNEY.

SAMSON'S STRENGTH DIDN'T COME FROM HIS HAIR, BUT IN HIS VOWS AND OBEDIENCE TO GOD. THE SCRIPTURE WILL ALLOW

US TO SEE THAT HIS SPIRITUAL BEING MADE HIM REMARKABLY STRONG. THE SPIRIT OF THE LORD CAME UPON SAMSON. THE MESSAGE WILL DEAL WITH THREE DIFFERENT SCRIPTURES IN THE 14 AND 15TH CHAPTER OF THE BOOK OF JUDGES. I WILL DEAL WITH THE 6TH AND 19TH VERSE IN CHAPTER 14 AND VERSE 14 IN THE 15TH CHAPTER. ALL THREE VERSUS HAVE ONE COMMON DENOMINATOR AND THAT IS THE PHRASE THE SPIRIT OF THE LORD CAME UPON HIM. IT WASN'T SAMSON'S PHYSICAL ATTRIBUTES THAT GAVE HIM POWER BUT THE SPIRIT OF THE LORD.

EVEN WITH THE SPIRIT OF THE LORD UPON HIS LIFE, SAMSON STILL ENDED UP IN A MESS. SOMETIMES WE CAN CAUSE HAVOC IN OUR OWN LIVES. OUR LIFE OFTEN BECOMES A MESS WHEN WE FAIL TO LEARN FROM OUR MISTAKES. THE OLD SAYING IS THAT A HARD HEAD MAKES A SOFT BEHIND. MAKING A MISTAKE ISN'T SO BAD, BUT WHEN WE DON'T LEARN FROM THESE MISTAKES WE ARE HEADED FOR HEARTACHE AND PAIN. WE OFTEN DO THIS AS CHRISTIANS WE MAKE POOR DECISIONS OR COMMIT A SIN AND ASK GOD FOR FORGIVENESS AND REPEAT THE SAME SIN. DOES THIS SOUND FAMILIAR? THIS WILL ONLY ENSURE ONE THING AND THAT IS THAT OUR LIVES WILL SOMEHOW END UP IN A MESS. I WOULD RATHER BUILD UP A GOOD SPIRITUAL FOUNDATION NOW, THAN REPAIR ONE LATER.

LIKE SO MANY OF US, THIS IS WHAT HAPPENED TO SAMSON. HE JUST DIDN'T SEEM TO LEARN FROM HIS MISTAKES. I WILL TAKE A LOOK AT SOME OF SAMSON'S LIFE THAT MAY SOUND FAMILIAR TO YOU AND I. FIRST OF ALL SAMSON HAD A BIG MOUTH. HE NEVER DID LEARN TO CHANGE THAT. IN THE FOURTEENTH CHAPTER OF JUDGES WE LEARN THAT SAMSON DECIDED TO GO AMONG THE PHILISTINES TO TAKE A WIFE. HE WENT THERE AGAINST THE ADVICE OF HIS PARENTS. DOES THIS SOUND FAMILIAR? WE OFTEN

DO THINGS THAT WE ARE FOREWARNED ABOUT FROM OUR PARENTS OR PASTOR. SAMSON HAD A WEAKNESS FOR BEAUTIFUL WOMEN. THE FLESH WANTS EVERYTHING THAT FEELS OR LOOKS GOOD TO IT, EVEN THOUGH IT MAY BE DETRIMENTAL TO THE SOUL. A LOT OF US HAVE WEAKNESSES FOR THINGS SUCH AS CARS, HOMES, WOMEN, MEN OR PLAIN OLD POPULARITY. SAMSON SAW A BEAUTIFUL WOMAN DOWN IN A LITTLE CITY CALLED TIMNAH THAT CAUGHT HIS EYE. THE DEVIL ALWAYS HAS SOMETHING THAT WILL CATCH OUR EYE THAT WE AREN'T SUPPOSE TO HAVE. WHEN SAMSON GOT DOWN TO THE CITY HE WANTED TO SHOW OFF A LITTLE BIT FOR THIS WOMAN THAT HE WAS TRYING TO IMPRESS, SO HE GAVE THE PHILISTINE MEN A RIDDLE. HE WAS THINKING BACK ON A LION THAT HE HAD KILLED AND HE MADE THE HONEY THE CATCH PHRASE TO THE RIDDLE. THE RIDDLE SAID "OUT OF THE EATER, SOMETHING TO EAT; OUT OF THE STRONG SOMETHING SWEET." HE GAVE THE MEN SEVEN DAYS TO ANSWER THE RIDDLE. ON THE FOURTH DAY THE PHILISTINE MEN WENT TO THE BEAUTIFUL WOMAN THAT SAMSON WAS COURTING TO TRY AND PERSUADE HER TO GET THE ANSWER OUT OF HIM. REMEMBER THIS WAS A WOMAN THAT SAMSON'S PARENTS HAD WARNED HIM TO STAY AWAY FROM. IF YOU DON'T REMEMBER ANYTHING ELSE OUT OF THIS MESSAGE REMEMBER TO BE FOREWARNED IS TO BE FOREARMED. SOMETIMES WHEN WE GET INVOLVED WITH SOMEONE ON PURE LOOKS INSTEAD OF SUSTENANCE WE DON'T KNOW HOW HE OR SHE WILL REACT UNDER PRESSURE. THE MEN WENT TO SAMSON NEW INTEREST AND TOLD HER TO FIND OUT THE ANSWER TO THE RIDDLE OR THEY WOULD BURN HER FAMILY'S HOUSE DOWN. SHE THREW HERSELF AT SAMSON, SOBBING AND CRYING TO PLAY UPON SAMSON'S WEAKNESS WITH HER WOMANLY WILES. SHE THEN BEGAN TO PLAY UPON SAMSON EMOTIONAL STATUS, AND TELL HIM THAT HE MUST

HATE HER AND THAT HE WAS TREATING HER LIKE THE PHILISTINE
MEN. SAMSON SHOULD HAVE KNOWN BETTER. HE WAS CHOSEN
FOR GREAT THINGS. HE DIDN'T KNOW WHO HE REALLY WAS IN GOD.
HE DOUBTED HIMSELF AND BEGAN TO PLEASE OTHERS SUCH AS
THIS BEAUTIFUL WOMAN WHOM HIS PARENTS HAD FOREWARNED
HIM ABOUT. YOU CAN GUESS WHAT SAMSON DID WHEN THIS
BEAUTIFUL WOMAN BEGAN TO PLEAD HER CASE. YOU ARE RIGHT,
HE OPENED HIS BIG MOUTH AND BEGAN TO SPILL THE BEANS.

SAMSON FOUND HIMSELF ASKING "HOW DID I GET MYSELF
IN THIS MESS".

SAMSON STILL DIDN'T LEARN FROM HIS MISTAKES HE FELL
FOR ANOTHER PHILISTINE WOMAN AND HER NAME WAS DELILAH.
THE SOLDIERS OF PHILISTINE COULDN'T CAPTURE OR DETERMINE
THE ROOT OF SAMSON'S STRENGTH SO THEY BEGAN TO COAX HIS
NEWFOUND WEAKNESS DELILAH. IT DIDN'T TAKE DELILAH LONG
TO GET TO THE SOURCE. SAMSON PLAYED AROUND A COUPLE OF
TIMES, BUT FINALLY REVEALED THE SOURCE OF HIS STRENGTH TO
DELILAH. HE TOLD HER THE SOURCE OF HIS STRENGTH WAS IN HIS
HAIR. SAMSON WAS LIKE SO MANY OF US; HE JUST COULDN'T KEEP
HIS MOUTH SHUT. HE ALSO SEEMED TO ALWAYS FIND HIMSELF
HANGING WITH THE WRONG CROWD. MY DAD USE TO TELL ME AS
A YOUNG MAN THAT IT WAS BETTER TO KEEP YOUR MOUTH SHUT
AND PEOPLE THINK YOU A FOOL, THAN TO SPEAK AND REMOVE ALL
DOUBT.

I CAN THINK BACK ON MY LIFE WHEN I'VE SAID THINGS
WHEN I WISH I HAD BEEN SILENT. I CAN ONLY THINK OF ONE OR
TWO TIMES WHEN I WAS SILENT AND WISH THAT I HAD SPOKEN UP.
OUR MOUTHS CAN GET US IN A WORLD OF TROUBLE. THE BIBLE
SAYS, "THERE IS LIFE AND DEATH IN THE TONGUE". A LOT OF US
WILL CRITICIZE OUR FELLOW MAN UNJUSTLY. WE LIKE TO SPREAD

GOSSIP WITHOUT REALIZING THAT WE ARE PLAYING RIGHT INTO THE DEVILS HAND. I WANT TO EQUIP YOU WITH SOME PERTINENT INFORMATION ABOUT FIGHTING THIS WARFARE THAT WE ARE IN TODAY. GOSSIP IS OF THE DEVIL. HE ALWAYS NEEDS A WITNESS TO GO AND SPREAD HIS VENOM. THINK ABOUT THAT FOR A WHILE. HOW WHEN WE SEE A FELLOW CHRISTIAN OR HUMAN BEING DO SOMETHING WRONG WE CAN'T WAIT TO TELL WHAT THEY DID OR WHAT WE THOUGHT HAPPENED. IT'S A WAY FOR THE DEVIL TO GET GLORY OUT OF A SAINT FALLING INTO SIN. AS BELIEVERS IN CHRIST WE ARE GOING TO HAVE TO LEARN TO CONTROL OUR MOUTHS.

ANOTHER AREA OF SAMSON'S LIFE THAT I WANT TO LOOK AT IS HIS TEMPER. HE HAD A VENGEFUL ATTITUDE. SAMSON COULDN'T CONTROL HIS TEMPER. THERE ARE FOUR CHAPTERS IN THE BIBLE THAT DEAL WITH SAMSON'S LIFE AND YOU CAN'T READ A HALF A DOZEN VERSUS WITHOUT SEEING HIM RISE UP IN ANGER. THIS CAUSED HIM MANY TRIBULATIONS. THIS IS THE REASON THAT HE OFTEN HAD TO ASK, "HOW DID I GET MYSELF IN THIS MESS"? IN CHAPTER 15 OF THE BOOK OF JUDGES YOU WILL READ HOW SAMSON FLIES OFF THE HANDLE AGAIN, WHEN HIS BRIDE IS GIVEN AWAY. HE GOES OUT AND CATCHES THREE HUNDRED FOXES, AND I MIGHT ADD THAT IS NO EASY TASK. SAMSON TOOK THE THREE HUNDRED FOXES AND LIGHTED TORCHES AND BROKE THE FOXES INTO PAIRS AND TIED THEIR TALES TOGETHER, THEN TOOK THEM OUT TO THE GRAIN FIELDS AND SET THEM ON FIRE SO THAT THEY WOULD BURN THE ENTIRE PHILISTINE CROP. THIS SOUNDS LIKE A LOT OF US, BUT THE LORD SAYS VENGEANCE IS HIS. WE OFTEN HAVE CHILDISH OR IMMATURE BEHAVIOR LIKE SAMSON. WE WANT TO GET JUSTICE FOR LOSING SOMETHING THAT WE PROBABLY SHOULDN'T HAVE HAD FROM THE VERY START. SAMSON ALWAYS HAD TO HAVE THE LAST WORD. HE ALWAYS HAD TO HAVE THE LAST

HIT. HIS TEMPER CAUSED HIM TO LOOSE A LOT OF THE BLESSINGS THAT HIS SPIRITUAL FOUNDATION WOULD HAVE RESTORED TO HIM ANYHOW. A TEMPER WILL OFTEN CAUSE YOU TO ASK THAT FAMOUS QUESTION OF "HOW DID I GET MYSELF IN THIS MESS"?

THE LAST AREA OF SAMSON'S LIFE THAT WE WILL LOOK AT IS LEARNING FROM PRIOR MISTAKES. THIS WILL BE PERTINENT TO THOSE IN WARFARE. THE BATTLE STARTS AND ENDS IN ONE'S MIND. WE HAVE TO HAVE CONTROL OVER THE MIND TO CONTROL THE HUMAN COMPLEXITIES OF OUR FRAILTIES, WHICH IS OUR FLESH OR OUR PHYSICAL DESIRES. SAMSON WAS PHYSICALLY STRONG BUT LIKE MANY OF US SPIRITUALLY WEAK. SAMSON WAS ALWAYS PLAYING THE OLD GAME OF SEEING HOW CLOSE HE COULD GET TO THE FIRE WITHOUT GETTING BURNED. SAMSON ALSO DIDN'T CHOOSE HIS ASSOCIATIONS WELL. WHEN WE CHOOSE THE WRONG FRIENDS OR ASSOCIATES WE WILL OFTEN FIND OURSELVES IN TROUBLE. ONCE AGAIN WE MIGHT FIND OURSELVES ASKING "HOW DID I GET MYSELF IN THIS MESS"?

SAMSON KEPT HANGING AROUND THE WRONG CROWD. HE KEPT ASSOCIATING AROUND WORLDLY PEOPLE SUCH AS THE PHILISTINES OF THAT TIME. HE DIDN'T TAKE CARE IN SELECTING A WIFE; HE WENT ON OUTER BEAUTY ONLY. I AM FORTUNATE TODAY TO HAVE A WIFE THAT IS JUST AS BEAUTIFUL ON THE OUTSIDE AS SHE IS ON THE INSIDE. IN A WAR YOU HAVE TO KNOW WHO YOU CAN DEPEND ON. TODAY I DEPEND ON JESUS CHRIST AND THOSE WHO ARE TRYING TO BE LIKE HIM, CHRISTIANS. RELATIONSHIPS ARE VERY POWERFUL. THEY ARE GOING TO LIFT US UP OR THEY ARE GOING TO PULL US DOWN. THAT'S WHY COMMUNING TOGETHER WITH A GROUP OF CHRISTIANS IN A CHURCH SETTING IS SO IMPORTANT IN WORSHIPPING THE LORD. IRON DOES SHARPEN IRON.

SECULAR AS WELL AS RELIGIOUS STUDIES SHOW THERE ARE A COUPLE OF DETERMINING FACTORS THAT WILL DETERMINE WHERE WE WILL BE IN THE NEXT FIVE YEARS.

1. THE BOOKS YOU READ WILL DETERMINE WHERE YOU WILL BE. (I SUGGEST STARTING WITH THE BIBLE)
2. THE PEOPLE YOU ASSOCIATE WITH IS THE SECOND DETERMINING FACTOR.

WHEN YOU ARE DETERMINING WHOM YOU SHOULD ASSOCIATE YOURSELF WITH YOU SHOULD SEE IF THAT PERSON HAS THE SAME PRIORITIES THAT YOU HAVE IN LIFE. SECOND YOU SHOULD LOOK AT HIS OR HER ATTITUDE. ATTITUDE WILL DETERMINE ONE'S ALTITUDE IN LIFE. ASK YOURSELF " HOW DO MY FRIENDS VIEW LIFE OR MAYBE A BETTER QUESTION WOULD BE TO ASK THEM HOW DO THEY THINK LIFE TREATS THEM". THERE ANSWER WILL BE A GOOD GAUGE. LIFE IS LIKE A BOOMERANG; IT COMES BACK TO US THE SAME WAY WE GIVE IT. THE NEXT CONCEPT IN PICKING ASSOCIATES IS TO SEE HOW THEY GET ALONG WITH OTHER PEOPLE. DO THEY BUILD OTHERS UP, OR ARE THEY ALWAYS TEARING SOMEONE DOWN?

SAMSON DIDN'T CHECK ANY OF THESE THINGS OUT, HE CONTINUOUSLY RAN WITH THE WRONG CROWD. SAMSON DIDN'T CONSULT WITH GOD BEFORE MAKING DECISIONS. HE DIDN'T TAKE GOD SERIOUS UNTIL HE WAS IN A MESS. IN A WAR, SUCH AS THE WARFARE THAT WE ARE ALL FACING WE HAVE TO TAKE GOD SERIOUS. THIS IS SERIOUS BUSINESS. LIFE OR DEATH! SAMSON LIVED FOR HIMSELF; HE THOUGHT HE COULD DO ANYTHING BECAUSE OF HIS PHYSICAL STRENGTH. HE HAD TO LEARN THE HARD WAY THAT IS FLESH ISN'T WHAT KEPT HIM STRONG IN A SPIRITUAL WAR. HE LEARNED THE HARD WAY THAT PRAYER IS THE KEY TO UNLOCKING OUR TRUE STRENGTH. HE WAS LIKE US HE

DIDN'T LEAN ON GOD UNTIL HE WAS ASKING HIMSELF " HOW DID I GET MYSELF INTO THIS MESS"?

I'M HERE AS A LIVING WITNESS TO TELL YOU WHEN YOU DO REALIZE THAT YOU ARE IN A MESS OR WAR AND CALL UPON THE NAME OF JESUS, HE WILL BE THERE. THE KEY IS NOT TO WAIT UNTIL IT IS TO LATE. SAMSON CALLED UPON JESUS IN JUST THE NICK OF TIME. HE WAS BEING USED AS A SIDESHOW. I THINK OF HOW MANY TIMES THE DEVIL HAS USED US AS HIS PERSONAL SIDESHOW, HIS PUPPET. CAN YOU IMAGINE THE LAUGH HE HAS WHEN WE DO SOME OF THOSE SILLY THINGS WHEN WE CLOUD OUR MIND WITH DRUGS AND ALCOHOL, OR OTHER WORLDLY THINGS THAT CLOUDS OUR JUDGMENT? SAMSON WAS BLINDED IN THE TEMPLE OF DAGON, AND THE PHILISTINES WERE IN HIGH SPIRITS, THEY SHOUTED "BRING OUT SAMSON TO ENTERTAIN US". THEY BROUGHT SAMSON OUT OF THE PRISON AND MADE HIM PERFORM FOR THEM, BUT AS THEY STOOD SAMSON ALONG THE PILLARS THAT SUPPORTED THE TEMPLE HE BEGAN TO THINK OF WHO HE WAS IN THE LORD. HE ASKED THE MEN TO PUT HIM WHERE HE COULD FEEL THE PILLARS, SO THAT HE COULD LEAN AGAINST THEM. CAN YOU IMAGINE ALL OF THE PEOPLE WATCHING THE SHOW, JUST WANTING SAMSON TO FAIL? DOES THIS SOUND FAMILIAR? I CAN IMAGINE THAT THERE ARE PEOPLE WHO WERE WAITING ON ME TO FAIL. ALL THE RULERS OF PHILISTINE WHERE THERE AND ON THE ROOF THERE WERE ABOUT THREE THOUSAND MEN AND WOMEN WATCHING. SAMSON REALIZED THAT HIS STRENGTH WASN'T IN HIS HAIR AT ALL, BUT REALIZED HIS STRENGTH WAS IN THE LORD. THE SPIRIT OF THE LORD CAME UPON SAMSON MIGHTILY AND WITH ONE BLOW HE BEGAN TO PULL THE PILLARS DOWN AND KILLED ALL OF HIS ENEMIES. SAMSON REALIZED THAT HE WASN'T WRESTLING AROUND WITH MEN BUT SPIRITUAL PRINCIPALITIES. HE OVERCAME

AND YOU CAN TOO! MAY THE SPIRIT OF THE LORD COME UPON YOU MIGHTILY IN WHATEVER PERSONAL WAR YOU MAY BE FIGHTING.

A DEAD-END SITUATION

SCRIPTURE: THE BOOK OF EXODUS 14TH CHAPTER 1ST THROUGH THE 16TH VERSE.

When we think about a dead-end situation, we usually think about being in a jam, in a fix, between a rock and a hard place. Some people may think of it as being from a poor family or becoming involved in teenage pregnancy. Some might think being in a dead-end situation means getting hooked on drugs and/or alcohol. Some might even think a dead-end situation is violence in the community or in our schools. Picture Erkle from Family Matters, who says he has fallen and he can't get up. To some that might be a bad situation.

There are many reasons why folks find themselves in a dead-end situation.Some reasons might be because of unwise decisions; some reasons may be because of because of unwise associations. Some might be because of domestic difficulties, or unwise financial decisions.

Some bad-end situations can be through no fault of your own. You can find yourself in a dead-end situation through the foolishness of others, but most likely, you get yourself into a dead-end situation because you are spiritually challenged. Whatever the reason for your bad situation, I have come to give some encouragement. There are some individuals reading this book right now who are in a bad situation, and this situation has been hounding them for quite some time. Let's look at the Word of God and gather some weapons to combat the wiles of the devil.

Let's take a look at some history: I want to go back to the Old Testament and begin to give you some basis of some people who were in a dead-end situation. I believe the story before us will help us learn some lessons on how to deal with a dead-end situation or just a bad situation. When we look at the passages in the Bible we see that the see that the people of God have found themselves in a deadly situation. I am here to tell you that they lived to tell about it, and if you will listen closely, if you will apply the lesions you have learned here in this book and hold on to God's unchanging hand, you will be able to survive any storm in your life. When you get into dead-end situations, when the lightening is flashing, when the thunder is roaring and the sea is raging all around you, don't quit! Young people don't throw in the towel. If you're at the end of your rope, tie a knot and hold on. Remember, bad situations only last for a season, and joy cometh in the morning. People might say Preacher you just don't understand what we go through today. You don't understand about coming from an underprivileged family; you don't understand me. You don't know how hard it is being me. You're right, I may not know you or your situation, but you have to ask yourself is your situation more serious than a dead Jesus behind a two ton rock, guarded by enemy soldiers? Is your problem any greater than a red sea when the enemy is chasing you? If not, I'm here to tell you that God is able to handle your situation. Jesus is a problem solver; He is away maker. When I'm in my prayer closet, I like to call him Jehovah Jireh, my provider. Sometimes when I'm not feeling my best, I like to call out Jehovah Ropha, my healer. Sometimes when my mind is at war with itself, I like to call out Jehovah Shalom, my peace giver. I want you to learn some lessons about life. There is nothing worse than to go through something and not learn anything from it. It is a terrible thing to come through a valley and not learn anything while you are down there. If you don't learn anything while you are down in the valley, you will not get to the mountain top. The first thing I want you to learn is that God wants us to have a personal reliance on him.

Let me give you a little background to the scripture. Israel had been in bondage for over 430 years, and during that time, they had adopted and internalized Egyptian values and morals. They began t fight like the Egyptians; they started to look like the Egyptians. As a matter of fact, other than in name, these Hebrew were Egyptians. They not only lived in Egypt, but Egypt began to live within them. I said all that to say that these Hebrews began to live by the standards of the world. How about you? Have you taken on the standards of the world? Can we tell you from the unsaved children? Have you set yourself apart? I read an article not too long ago on A.C. Green of the Los Angeles Lakers. Here is a man thirty-six years old, playing professional sports, who had set himself apart from the world. A.C. was a virgin at the age of thirty-six. He had saved himself for his life long companion. Let me tell you what he said in the article that impressed me. He said he placed his focus on walking with Christ first. Second, he kept thinking about reaching his goals, but his third comment is what stuck with me as most important. Young people, he said "I will not compromise or negotiate my beliefs." What a testimony, what a dedication and commitment to God? Can you say the same? What about us? Can our beliefs be compromised or negotiated? Do we put our reliance on the

Lord? The children of Israel had not learned to rely upon the Lord; they were walking by sight and not by faith, so God had to gain their attention. Sometimes when you turn your back on God, he has to get your attention. That is why sometime we end up in a dead-end situation. The children of Israel were on a dead-end street. I know this because geography teaches us that on the north was a massive mountain, to the south was the sweltering heat of the desert, to the east was Goshen and Ramses where they had just left with Pharaoh's horses and chariots right on their tail. In front of them was that watery grave called the Red Sea. They were trapped. They were in a dead-end situation.

You might ask yourself how they got themselves into a dead-end situation sometimes; we can get there by no fault of our own. Sometime God has to put us through something to make us somebody. He has to continuously put us on the potter's wheel to make us what He wants us to be. We have to realize that this walk with Christ isn't all peaches and cream. The devil has a job, and I need for you to know what it is. His job is to come as a roaring lion, walking about this earth seeking to devour you. He wants to kill you.

It is as simple as that. So, don't think this Christian walk is going to be easy. I don't want you to be discouraged because help is only a prayer away. When we look at verse 10 in the scripture, it tells us that the children of Israel cried out unto the Lord. As you read up to this point you will not find the people had cried out to God until this time. God had brought them to a place where they had no one else to call upon but Him. Sometime in life, we want to try to figure things out; we want to follow our own rationale, our own reasoning. We want to depend upon our own intellect; we want to figure our own way out, but God says when you begin to walk in the flesh and not by faith, you will end up in a dead-end situation. When they found themselves in a dead-end situation, what they needed to have learned was to rely upon the Lord. No matter what trial or tribulation, rely on the Lord.

The Lord we serve will not forsake you, and he will never fail you! As the old song says take your burdens to the Lord and leave them there. The Lord requires your personal reliance upon him. The second lesson is a lesson of obedience to Him. The Lord tells Moses to instruct the people and Moses say to them "Stand Still", and he says unto them "see the salvation of the Lord". If you are not careful you will not hear the voice of God, and you will be walking around in disobedience rather than obedience. When they got between the devil and the Red sea, they began to start pointing fingers at one another. Oh, I know that doesn't happen to any of us today. We don't begin to blame everything and everyone around us for our own troubles. The key is not to get excited when we are in a dead-end situation. There are times we begin to lose control. I'm here to tell you the control was never ours to begin with. Moses had said to the people, these are things you need to do if you are going to learn to be obedient to the Lord. First of all, you need to stop having fear, fear is paralyzing. Fear will make you act like a fool. He says "do not fear, just trust God". Second Moses tells us to stand still. That's a big part of our problem today; we are doing too much. We don't like to stand still. We don't like to wait for God to show us his hand.

Martin Luther King once said, "We must learn to successfully deal with finite trouble without losing infinite hope". In other words, Dr. King was telling us to learn to not to focus so much on the problem because we will lose sight of who the problem solver is. If you keep focusing on your trouble, your trouble will only get larger, and you will make God seem smaller; but if you focus on God, he will get bigger and your problem will get smaller. So, Moses told the people to stand still. After all, you can't do anything anyhow. We need to be still and let Jesus take over the wheel.

Let Jesus drive for a little while!

After Moses directs them to not fear and stand still, he told them to wait and see the salvation of the Lord; see the deliverance of the Lord. We have to stop the lip service. True, it is possible to honor God with our mouths, but it's a shame to talk the talk and not walk the walk. Parents this part is for you. These young people are watching you. They are reading your life as if it were the Bible. What do they read? It doesn't matter how loud you shout, it doesn't matter how well you do the Holy dance, and it doesn't matter how much you come to church; if the book that these children are reading tells a different story than your lip service is providing. Would these children say that you are the same sanctified; holy-ghost filled Christian that they see today here in church. If not, you have become an ineffective witness for Jesus Christ.

I want you to remember some things. I want you to remember to rely on God, not your own understanding. Be obedient to God's word. Do not compromise or negotiate your beliefs. My final point is stand still and wait on the Lord. Your help doesn't come from the east or the west, but lift your eyes toward the hills from whence cometh your help. I tell you, if you fight the fight yourself, you will have to fight again, but if you let God fight your battles, you won't have to deal with it no more, ever. Scripture tells us it is final.

In every dead-end situation that God has resolved for you, there lie some hidden treasures. Sometime it just may be to increase your faith.

Faith an act of obedience, faith is acting like something is so when it is not in order for it to be so. What I am trying to tell you is to put your trust in the Lord, He will turn your dead-end situation into hidden treasures. Look at Moses as he stretched forth his rod, and they walked forward on dry land. They walked across the Red Sea and their feet didn't even get wet. You might be going through something in your life, but all you need to do is lean on and depend upon God. I am a living witness that the Lord can bring you out of a "Dead-end" situation.

NOW, WHO

IS.

L

DON'T QUIT   HELP IS ON THE WAY

<u>SCRIPTURE:</u> MATTHEW 15:21-28

There was a woman in the bible whose child was grievously vexed with a devil. There are many of us sitting right here whose children are vexed with the devil. There is a spirit of murder running rampant throughout the United States. There are demonic spirits of drugs and alcohol that are plaguing our young people. The devil is running through our streets as a roaring lion seeking to devour Christians whether they are young or old. We have the spirit of fornication that is vexing the children of God, a spirit that is causing teenage pregnancy and unwed mothers to be on the rise. There is a spirit of suicide in the midst of our people. People are taking their own lives at an alarming rate. These are just some of the most notable demonic spirits roaming the earth. The demonic spirit that I'm here to tell you about is a give-up spirit, a spirit that will cause one to lack endurance. When I looked up the word endurance I found that it means to put up with a strain, suffering or hardship. Did you realize that this is a learned behavior? What is the world learning from us as Christians? Do they see us give up when a situation becomes too hard?

Do they see us give up when the pastor ask us to do something that we may not want to do, or that we just don't understand? Our flesh will tell us that a situation is too hard for us, that we can't endure. Our flesh will even tell us that we can't endure an entire church service. It does this because the devil realizes there is something that we are in need of during the end part of the service. Something that will prepare us for the warfare that we are facing, or the battle that we will have to endure at another time. From now on, I want you to stand still, don't move or leave the service. Do what you have to do to endure the service until the end. This is a thinking message, a message with a lot of personal questions that we must ask ourselves in order to endure the trials of life. How do we handle suffering or hardship? I need you to realize the world may not be reading the bible but they are certainly reading how you handle yourself in times of hardship. Do they see the same person that we see on Sunday mornings?

We have to start training our children for the trials of life. The bible says, "train up a child in the way he should go: and when he is old, he will not depart from it". My father taught me to finish whatever I started. It didn't matter if it was something so simple as a game of basketball. I didn't realize it then, but I do now. He was instilling a spirit of endurance in my life. Throughout my journey with Jesus Christ, my worse fear is the Lord telling me that I did run well, but what did hinder me from the truth. If we get really honest with ourselves we will come to the conclusion that the majority of the time it is our own self that hindered us from doing the will of God. I often stop myself from accomplishing all that God has for me.

When I think of endurance I think of the Syrophonecian woman in the bible. She had left her country, her land, her family, all that was

84

important to her to seek God. I think of how hard her journey must have been, but she endured all the rigorous travels to make contact with Jesus. I think of how she must have been at her wit's end. How she was nearing her breaking point, but she knew if she could somehow hold on and not quit that her help was on the way. Can you imagine when she had traveled all this way to see Jesus, and when she called on his name, he answered her not a word. I think most of us would have thrown in the towel right there, but she was determined to receive help from Jesus. She needed deliverance for her daughter. It makes me think of how the disciples weathered the storm to get to the other side. How Job didn't quit because he knew that Jesus was his help. How Daniel endured the trials of the lion's den. The thing I think about the most is how Jesus endured the cross so that we can have eternal life. Imagine how they beat Jesus, ridiculed and called him names. Imagine being beat with the cat of nine tails, taking thirty-nine lashes, carrying that heavy cross and enduring all that pain for the cause of love.

We have got to get back to some basics. We have to instill a don't-quit-spirit in ourselves. If you begin to feel like you are at the end of your rope, tie a knot and hold on. Know that God is there and in control of every situation. Parents don't let your children quit anything in life, whether it is school, jobs, or anything that is good for them. Remember there is always a lesson when we have to endure a struggle. A good principle to learn in life is that when you walk down in the valley you are learning something that will help you to maintain your position when you get to the mountaintop. Struggles often prepare a person for success. When you read the biographies of great people, most of them have one thing in common and that is a struggle to make it to the top. Without the struggle they wouldn't have been ready for the blessing that God has given them. In my household it is a must to finish anything that we start. My son, thinks that I am being hard on him sometimes, well I am. Sometimes we will be playing a play station game and he will be losing. He will want to quit, but I always make him finish the game. This is preparing him to finish whatever life throws at him.

I want him to have the same endurance that the Syrophonecian woman had. She had the spirit of faith and endurance. She believed as long as she didn't give up, that Jesus would do his part. I have come to find out in life if we do our part we don't have to worry, God will certainly do his part. Even when the disciples came to discourage the woman, she wouldn't give up. Can you imagine this lady, traveling from a far off land, calling upon Jesus and he answered her not a word, then she fought her way through the disciples and when Jesus did answer her, he didn't give her the reply she wanted. What do you do, when you call upon Jesus and he answers you not a word? Then when he does, it's not the reply you want? You have to know that the Master is in control. You have to stand still and wait upon God. When God answered the woman he told her some things about herself. Jesus answered the woman and said, "I am not sent but unto the lost sheep of the house of Israel. A lot of us would have been ready to quit, but this amazing lady didn't give up she began to get serious with her plea to the Lord. She put all protocol away, she no longer cared who was around and listening she began to holler, "Lord help". That's what we need to do is take our pride and throw it in the garbage and begin to seek the Lord with all of our heart and soul. Cry out to the Master "Lord Help"!

I remember when I was down in the mire clay so far, that I imagine Jesus probably had to roll up his sleeve to get me out. I had nowhere else to turn, but to Jesus. I had tried everything that I could think of on my own, but I couldn't get myself out of the mess that I had created. We have to realize that we can't fight this spiritual warfare by ourselves it takes Jesus. I know for myself I didn't have time for any ceremonial routine. I was going to die and surely go to hell. I needed help. I didn't know if I was in order or out of order but I didn't want to die a drug addict, thief and liar. I had a choice to make that day, Heaven or Hell. I choose life and called out "Lord Help"! I would ask you today, is your choice heaven or hell. If the Lord came back today would you be sitting in the smoking or the non-smoking section?

We have got to get some endurance when in this warfare of life. The endurance of someone like the Syrophonecian woman, her story goes on to tell us that she must have been at her wits end. When she called out to Jesus Lord help, he replied and told her that "its not meet to take the children's bread and cast it to the dogs". I have to tell you most of us would have been furious, we would have said who does that Jesus think He is calling me a dog. Some so-called Christians might have even cursed our Lord and Savior out. Some might have thought I have come all this way and He is talking to me like that, but not her she humbled herself and said "Lord Truth". She had endurance and humility. She knew Jesus was her only hope. The devil would have loved to see her endure all the trials and obstacles she had overcome and quit without getting a healing for her daughter. How many times have we almost gotten a healing or miracle and quit just before the miracle happened? We have to realize our time and our ways aren't God's time and ways. We just have to keep moving and have faith. Our help doesn't come from the east or the west but from Jesus. We have to know that he is omnipotent and omnipresent. He has every situation under control. We have to get on a mission for the Lord.

After all of the trials and tribulations the Syrophonecian woman she answered the Lord with humility and told him he was telling the truth that she was unworthy of God's blessing, but that even the dogs could eat the crumbs from the Master's table. How many of you know that crumbs of a blessing from God can sustain and make us whole. Just a crumb from the master's table can set us free from drug and alcohol addiction, can cure cancer, restore a marriage, heal an unstable mind, give the moral-less morals and sustain you through any storm of life. God is Jehovah-Jireh a provider in the midst of any storm. He is Jehova-Shalom the giver of peace; He is Jehovah-Ropha a healer of any disease or affliction. He is the Lilly of the valley. God tells us in Matthew 10:22, "he that endures till the end shall be saved". The Lord is telling us don't quit, never give up--- Help is on the way! The devil has come to kill, steal and destroy, but Jesus has come that we may have life and have it more abundantly. When the devil comes stalking, you just keep on walking. God has made us some promises. If we endure we will be saved. Look at what God told Abraham in Hebrews 6:15 He said, "If he endured, if he hung in their with him, he would surely bless him". Don't give up before the miracle happens.

We have to position ourselves for our blessings. God will not bless a mess. So get your house in order. The Lord has begun a good work within you, so don't quit, let God finish this work until the end. Recognize that God is there even when you don't feel him. That's is a point that I want to make to you, this war isn't about emotions. It's about knowing your relationship with God. Instill his word in your heart and you will be ready for battle. Instilling the word of God is key to building endurance. Look at the Syrophonecian woman, scripture tells us that the woman's endurance caused her to be victorious, and that you can also be victorious in your endeavors in life. The lady endured hardship, she didn't quit, she kept her eye on Jesus, and he said to her, "Woman Great is thy faith: Be it unto thee even as it thou wilt, and her daughter was made whole from that very hour". The key to this lady's story was that she pursued God, she didn't quit, and she knew Jesus was her help. I want you to know that quitters never win and winners never quit.

Not too long ago I was grievously vexed with the demonic spirit of drugs and alcohol. I was a man with no character, no morals or values, but through the prayers of the righteous I was able to make contact with Jesus and I too was healed from that very moment. So to the parents of someone hooked on drugs or alcohol or if the devil has stolen your child, don't dare give up on them, call on the name of Jesus. If you don't remember any other slogans I use write this one down. It is an awful thing to be lost, but it's a terrible thing to be lost and have no one looking for you. Don't quit, you or your loved one's can be saved through Jesus Christ. Just holler "Lord Help"!

THAT BELONGS TO ME AND I WANT IT BACK!

<u>SCRIPTURE:</u>   1 SAMUEL 29TH & 30TH CHAPTERS

I will be coming from the 8th verse of chapter 30 of the book of Samuel----And David inquired of the Lord, saying, "shall I pursue after the troops? Shall I overtake them? And the Lord answered him, pursue: For thou shall surely overtake them and without fail, recover all". Have you ever lost something that belonged to you? Have you ever felt like something was stolen from you or something was lacking in your life. Have you ever felt that you were supposed to succeed at something but still failed? Have you ever felt like you missed an opportunity? If so you are in the right place today. I am going to give you some simple instructions into fulfilling your destiny.

I'm going to begin by giving you some biblical principals that one of the greatest men in the bible learned to use through many trials and tribulations. This man is David. He was a man that was after God's own heart. I won't go into all of the intricate details, but I do want to give you some hope and encouragement. I want to begin to destroy the devices or yokes that the devil has put into your life.

This man David, who in his childhood had slain the Giant Goliath, had become a little hard headed. Does this sound familiar in your own story? This is a story of someone that knew God's magnificent power, but still strayed from the ways of God. David began to remove himself from the covering of God and move on his own insight and understanding of the world. We must be careful to never move in the natural but always in the spiritual, in God's realm. David got so entangled in life's many traps that he forget who he served. He had a lapse of faith. He stepped out of the will of God. When we step out of God's will, things will get out of hand. We have to be cautious when we start maneuvering through life on our own understanding. Remember God's ways are different from our ways. His thinking is above our comprehension. David had become discouraged because of Saul's determination to kill him. I think sometimes we get discouraged when the enemy is trying to kill us, but remember that's his job. Know that and know it well. We are in a war. David should have known first hand being a soldier himself that the enemy's job is to try to destroy us, now I'm not saying that Saul was the enemy because he was a great man himself, but he and David had conflict. My analogy is concerning the enemy being the devil, who has come to steal, kill and destroy. The thing that David should have gathered from all the miraculous works that God had performed on David's behalf should have caused him to have an abundance of faith. He should have known by now to stand still and let God lead our path into battle. David did like most of us do, he began to move on his own insight rather than seek the advice of God. David left Israel asking God what to do. God hadn't told David to leave Israel, just like He hasn't told many of us to do the things we have done. A lot of times we are so busy conjuring up what we think God is saying, we miss what He is really trying to tell us. David had left Israel and gone over into the country of Philstia. He had become friends with the King of Gath. A great war began to break out and David found himself in an awkward situation. Is't funny when we don't seek God, how many times we will find ourselves in an awkward situation. He was out of God's plan. David was going to make a terrible mistake. He had taken his men over in Aphek. He was preparing them for war against his own people.

Did you know when you're not living holy and with integrity that you will develop stinking thinking? God's grace saved David from making a terrible mistake. A lot of times God will have divine intervention and step in when we are going to make a mistake that will harm what we are predestined to do or even be. The word of God tells me that; "God's grace is sufficient for us, for our strength is made perfect in weakness. If we would only realize that we aren't in this warfare alone. If we as human beings could just admit the weaknesses of our human frailties we wouldn't have to endure all of the unnecessary punishments of life. One thing is certain when we step out of the will of God, heartache and pain is sure to follow. I think you get the jest of it by now.

David had lost faith and began to move on his own understanding. He didn't wait on God to show him his hand. In the spiritual warfare that you will face through life you will have to ask yourself; did I wait on God to show me his hand or did I move forward on my own accord?

David had moved forward on his own accord, and while he was out somewhere he wasn't suppose to be, trouble was happening at home. His lack of faith caused him to lose some of the Gifts and the hedge of protection that God had given him. The prophet Isaiah said, "that if we are willing and obedient, that we shall eat the good of the land, but if we refuse and rebel, we shall be devoured by the sword; the mouth of God has spoken this". I have to tell you God loves praise and worship, but He requires obedience.

David's lack of faith caused him to lose some of his possessions. How many times in life has your lack of faith caused you to lose something or someone? Have you ever made a move out of haste later to find that God was just about to move on your behalf but you moved, and He couldn't bless you, and instead of being blessed you went through turmoil. When we look at our scripture text we find that David had returned to Philistia, the Amalekites had invaded Ziklag and had burned it down. Their wives, sons and daughters had been taken into captivity. **A** lot of times we put those we love into captivity through moving out of the realm of God. We are off somewhere we have no business being and the enemy moves in to capture our loved ones. I will say it again we are in a war, and the devil is looking to sift us as wheat. He wants to steal, kill and destroy you. David had gotten distressed; as a matter of fact his men had begun to talk about stoning him. This sound like modern day Christians and just people in general. David made a mistake and his men were ready to have his head. How many of you know that when you make a mistake, your followers aren't as forgiving **as Jesus?** Sometimes the Lord will allow us to fall flat on our face so that we can remember just whom we serve. I once heard a preacher say that we can get on our knees two ways, one to thank God for all his goodness or two get on our knees to ask for mercy and help. I would much rather Thank him for His grace.

This brings me to the meat of the text. David had come to his senses and remembered where his help came from. David remembered when praises go up, blessings come down. When everyone else began to throw in the towel, David remembered the goodness and mercy of the Lord. David began to encourage himself. This is something that we are going to have to learn to do when in battle. Sometimes it only takes a scripture, song or sermon to instill faith in your heart during times of trouble. Today I always keep the word of God near and dear to my heart, especially in case of an emergency.

When David had gotten back to his senses and realized that his help didn't come from east or the west, but from the Lord. I imagine he stated doing that holy dance that he sometimes did. I imagine he began to sing praises of joy. I imagine a couple of Psalms came from this trials and tribulations. David went into a secret place with the Lord and began to worship Him. He began to inquire of the Lord. He asked the Lord what should he do. This is what we have to do to get out of our self and get into Jesus. David asks the Lord if he should pursue after his enemy. Let me break it down for you a little further. When we have moved out of the realm of God, we have to get on our knees and ask God for forgiveness, so that our prayers won't be blocked from heaven. When we have lost our family due to drugs, alcohol, extra-marital affairs or if our indiscretions have caused us to be an ineffective witness for Christ. We must repent! We must seek God for the answers to our restoration. You can walk through any neighborhood and see lost souls, lost property and businesses that belong to us as Christians. Just look on television and you will see something that should be ours. We need to claim those things in the name of Jesus, with our main purpose being to build the army of the Lord. It is time for us to get out of this great huddle of life and start to play the game with some enthusiasm. We are on the winning team and it's about time that we acted like it. We have got to put some action behind these great messages that we are receiving from our Pastors Sunday after Sunday. We have to put an end to losing our children to this world that we live in today. God is telling us to seek his righteousness, his holiness, and His spirit. We are going to have to listen for His voice and know the difference between His voice and a pork chop dream. If we just begin to listen to God closely we can hear him say, "Whom shall I send, and who will go". Are we going to say here I am Lord, use me to go and get those things back which we have lost due to sin". We are going to have to be bold soldiers for the Lord, and cry out to the world, that belongs to me and I want it back!

Scripture tells us that as David began to inquire of the Lord, he began to seek God, and he waited for God to answer him. God will answer when we seek him. Scripture tells us to seek and we shall find, to knock and the door will be answered. His word is never void. God can't lie. If you seek you will find a resolution to your problem. All we have to do is begin to live holy and with integrity and God will do the rest. God is telling us to pursue, and we shall surely overtake the devil without fail. We will recover all! This is a simple bible principle that is telling us that we have some rights as children of God. God tells us if He be for us, who can be against us? Don't you know that the love of God can conquer all?

We have to take our communities back from the devil. We have to lead that drug dealer, whoremonger, and adulterer back to Jesus. This is a must if we are to keep this country from the perils of hell. We need to put our country back in the hands of Christians and take it out of the hands of unsaved politicians. We need to take back businesses that rightfully belong to us. God has a thousand cattle on a hillside, and as Christians we should not want for anything. I am a living witness that you can recover your life without fail, no matter how hard it may seem. I walked with the devil and did everything I thought I was big and bad enough to do, and he turned on me. The devil's only plan is to sift you like wheat as I mentioned earlier. I implore you to turn from a negative attitude and lifestyle so that God can restore you to your rightful place. God can and will deliver! You shall recover all without fail!

NEVER LOOK BACK

GENESIS 19:15-19,26

I have come here this to tell you that the bible says "To every thing there is a season, and a time to every purpose under the heaven: ² A time to be born, and a time to die; a time to plant, and a time to pluck up that which is planted; ³ A time to kill, and a time to heal; a time to break down, and a time to build up; ⁴ A time to weep, and a time to laugh; a time to mourn, and a time to dance; ⁵ A time to cast away stones, and a time to gather stones together; a time to embrace, and a time to refrain from embracing; ⁶ A time to get, and a time to lose; a time to keep, and a time to cast away; ⁷ A time to rend, and a time to sew; a time to keep silent, and a time to speak; ⁸ A time to love, and a time to hate; a time of war, and a time of peace.

The purpose of this book is to declare war on the devil. We as a body of Christians are calling him out in the name of Jesus. I want to tell the devil. We are no longer your victim, but are victorious in the name of Jesus. We aren't taking the devils mess any more. He has no more dominion or rule over us. We want the devil to know that to that we are still standing. We have survived.

America has become the modern day Sodom and Gamorrah. Look at some of the similarities going on in the U.S. today. Homosexuality is on the rise. They are trying to compare themselves to minorities that have had to overcome the oppressions or stigmas that the American system has placed on a group of people because of their ethnicity or color of one's skin. I can not choose what color I am, but I can certainly choose the lifestyle that I'm going to live. I declare war on any negative attitude or lifestyle. Homosexuals are trying to change the wording of the constitution when it comes to marriages. The main biblical purpose of marriage is to pro-create. I'm here to tell you that a man and a man or a woman and a woman can't create life. I would therefore have to ask what is the purpose of this union. As a matter of fact, in the bible a whole city was destroyed for these immoral acts. When I look at the text it tells me even when Lot was in a state of sin, he wouldn't let the angel be sodomized by homosexual acts.

In Sodom a lot of the same things were taking place that are plaguing our society today. The lifestyles are parallel. They were plagued with such immoral living such as alcohol and drug abuse. These are tools of the devil to capture one's mind. A distorted mind is the primary weapon of choice for Satan. Drugs and alcohol are mood-altering substances. They can change one's predestination in the blink of an eye. These substances can cause one to miss what God has intended for them and let the world get in the way. Drugs and alcohol have caused more men to be incarcerated than any other factor. There are more Black men incarcerated, than there are living in the middle-income level of society.

The question of the day would be, what do we do? Once we have gotten out of a situation such as drugs, alcohol or any other bad situation. One of the key things to remember comes from the text which God tells Lot never to look back at his old lifestyle in Sodom and Gamorrah. When God has delivered you from the pits of Hell, why look back. Looking back is a trick of the enemy. Old slew foot is only going to let you see a distorted picture of the past experiences when you were his prisoner of warfare. He is only going to let you see half the movie. This means he will only let you see the portion of the experience that was pleasurable to your flesh. He let's you see the lights flashing, the smell of the perfume, the distinct odor of the drug or alcohol, the concubines of the devil, meaning the women and sounds of a good party. He never let's you see yourself destroying your marriage, going to jail, or losing your job. He only let's you see half the movie. I beg you if you ever think about the old lifestyle that you have come out of always play the videotape the entire way through. This will discourage you from ever going back to where God has delivered you. I assure you that you aren't missing anything from that old life of sin. The problem is that we often don't forgive ourselves. We try to punish ourselves. We try to pay the price for our sins. I am here to tell you that you are only inviting sin back into your life. Why try and pay for something that Jesus has already paid the price for. He died upon the cross for the remission of our sins.

God gives us some clear examples throughout the bible, where he has delivered men and women out of terrible situations. Look at the man with palsy, Jesus tells the man " Arise and walk, but that ye may know that the Son of man hath power on earth to forgive sins, then he said to the sick of the palsy, arise take up thy bed and go unto your house". The

Lord never once told the man to go back and look at his sinful life but to move forward. Another story in the bible is the woman who anointed the Messiah with oil at Simon the Lepers house; Jesus said to her "Wherefore I say unto thee her sins, which are many are forgiven, for she loved much: but to whom little is forgiven, the same loveth little. And He said unto her, thy sins are forgiven. And they sat at meat with Him and began to say within themselves, who is this that forgiveth sin also? And he said to the woman thy faith have saved thee go in peace". What Jesus was telling the woman and is telling us today, is that He sees something in us, such as our faith on the day we called His name and we were delivered. So why look back. God has pardoned our life of sin. Never look back at where we came from only move forward in the name of Jesus. The Lord is telling us that we are forgiven, so we must learn to forgive ourselves. A lot of our problems lie within our flesh and mind. There is something about that old sinful life that the flesh misses. Sin feels good to the flesh. It likes anything that makes it feel good, but I have to forewarn you that what feels good to the flesh is often destructive to the spirit. It felt so good to some of us that we had to be drug out of our personal Sodom and Gomorrah like Lot and his family. We didn't have enough sense to come out of a painful situation on our own. It took the divine intervention of Christ himself. If it weren't for the prayer warriors and angels placed in our lives we would still be stuck in a stage of torment. I know for me God had to role up his sleeve and pull me out of the mire clay. Instead of looking back we should be praising and worshipping God for this mighty feat. If God has paid the price, why do we insist on looking back at our old condition or state of mind? Jesus has already paid that debt. He was wounded for our transgression, bruised for our iniquities, the chastisement of our peace was upon him and we have been healed by his stripes, so why look back. Never look back. The only thing you need to know about the past is that God brought you through that situation and He can bring you through whatever situation you may be encountering now. Andre Crouch once said," if I never had any problems, I would have never known that God could solve them". As Christians our problem is that we think we aren't suppose to go through trials and tribulations. The bible says "beloved think it not strange concerning the fiery trial which is to try you, as though some strange thing happened unto you: But rejoice, inasmuch as ye are partaker of Christ's sufferings; that, when his glory shall be revealed ye may be glad also with exceedingly joy. We have to be prepared for this walk with Jesus; it's not an easy road to toll. The trick is not to look back; the devil wants you to wallow in shame and pity. He will only allow you to see bits and pieces of what actually took place in your suffering. It is a funny thing how easily the mind and flesh will let you forget the pain and suffering you have endured. I don't know what it is about that, but I am sure of one thing it's a battle of the mind.

When I was a drug addict the devil would only allow my mind to see half of the situation or tape, as I call it the video of my life. As I said before don't look back once God has delivered you from something. I don't know how many times in my ministry I have seen marriages destroyed because the devil convinces one of the spouses to keep looking back at one of the indiscretions of their mate. This causes a division in the marriage and the mind to be in a state of torment. The devil will fill your head with all kinds of thoughts. Thoughts that aren't even yours. He will only let you see how bad your marriage was, he wants you to destroy this sacrament because it is one of the strongest weapons of Christ, a man and a woman coming together to serve the Lord, to bring others to salvation. I implore you never to look back once God has restored your marriage. If God has forgiven a situation and put it in the sea of forget we have to do the same. If you do not move forward a tremendous battle will take place in the mind. We will begin to imagine and focus in on a lot of things that aren't even reality. That is what the devil thrives on, confusion. If he can cause confusion in a marriage he can begin to affect all kinds of things. God has healed people from all kinds of past situations, child molestation, drug addiction, adultery in a marriage and an array of dreadful things but we don't allow God to heal us because we keep looking back.

God has some promises for you. The bible is a contract for life. It is the deed and title to the land. It is Jesus' last will and testament. He has even put it in writing for you. Remember when He was in the garden and the devil tempted Him with food and God said it is written, Man shall not live by bread alone, but by every word that proceedeth out of the mouth of God. You got it in writing that if we confess our sins, he is faithful and just to forgive us *our* sins, and to cleanse us from all unrighteousness. God is telling you something. You are a child of the King. He has a purpose for you; you have to move forward with the plan of God and stop looking back at that old life. It's a trick of the enemy.

It is written that His grace is sufficient for thee: for your strength is made perfect in weakness. Most gladly therefore will I take glory in my infirmities, for Christ's sake: for when I am weak, then am I strong. Have you ever noticed that when things aren't going our way, that's when our anointing is the strongest. When you were in your own personal Sodom and Gomorrah God had your undivided attention. It is written in His word that when we have the sentence of death in ourselves, which is sin, that we shouldn't trust ourselves, but in God, which raiseth the dead.

God promises you some things as His heir. It is written that once you have come out of sin that you should be the head and not the tail. You should be above and not beneath. God goes on further to tell you that you will become the lender of money and not the borrower of money.

His word says, "That if you are willing and obedient that you will have the goodness of the land".

It is written "that if you are in the law of the LORD; and in his law doth you meditate day and night. [3] You shall be like a tree planted by the rivers of water, that bringeth forth his fruit in his season; his leaf also shall not wither; and whatsoever you do shall prosper". With all this in mind I have to ask you again why would you look back?

Some of the reasons people look back are because they don't realize what is written and the promises of God. I implore you to start reading the word of God and instill it in your heart. You will need it to put on the entire armor of God. It will ensure that your armor is shiny and that it doesn't have any cracks or holes in it. This is important when going through spiritual warfare.

The bible says "Therefore if any man *be* in Christ, *he is* a new creature: old things are passed away; behold, all things are become new". For some reason we insist on looking back, because the devil tricks us, we don't feel new. I have often heard people say that I'm saved but I don't feel saved. This is a definite trick of the enemy. It is a mind game. If you haven't got it by now, know this whole battle is in our mind. Once you know that, you will know how to combat the wiles of the devil. Don't fight him on your own, take Jesus to the forefront of the battle.

You have to know what is in your contract. Jesus already paid for your sins. He took thirty-nine lashes, was beat with the cat of nine tails that tore his skin and ripped it as if it were paper . God put it in writing that "he was the resurrection and the life: he that believeth in Him, though he were dead, yet shall he live: [26] And whosoever liveth and believeth in Jesus shall never die". One thing about God he put it in writing for us, He gave us a contract or a guide to live by so that we can live holy and with integrity. We have got to get tougher! We are going to have to learn to endure some things. We need to endure hardness as a good soldier for Jesus Christ.

Let me tell you some things that are not in the bible:

It doesn't say you have to let your marriage fail.

It doesn't say you have to stay hooked on drugs or alcohol.

It doesn't say that you have to let the devil rule over you.

It doesn't say that you have to wallow in self-pity.

It doesn't say that you have to have an unstable mind concerning things of past, present or future, but he promises you a sound mind.

You have got to realize some things. You have to know God will not lie or forsake you. You are His child, you have been adopted by Him. David said, "I was young but now I'm old, and I have never seen the righteous forsaken, nor his seed begging breed".

Never look back! Joseph summed it up for you when he said, "What the devil meant for bad, God transformed it for your good."

In closing with this story I want to tell you some specific things out of our text in the book of Genesis. The city of Sodom and Gomorrah was to be destroyed and God had sent some angels to tell Lot. Lot had been living among sinners and in sin for some time. He had become comfortable living this negative lifestyle. It had caused some damage, especially in his ability to witness. Lot had gone to tell his son-in-laws that the city would be destroyed and they didn't believe him because his credibility was damaged. God can restore your credibility, but I'm here to tell you if you keep going back to the same old lifestyle it will become harder and harder to repair, so once out of sin, stay out of sin. Secondly, Lot had become so accustomed to sin he didn't want to leave that condition. Remember the longer you stay in sin the harder it is to leave sin. So get out and stay out! Once out of sin never look back, only move forward. The bible goes on to tell us that Lot's wife looked back and she became a pillar of salt. Never Look Back at the old sinful life God has brought you from, only move forward with your new challenges of living holy with integrity.

HOW TO DEVELOP A FAITHFUL MAN

SCRIPTURE: HEBREWS 11:1-6

In society today, we are lacking faithful men. We are lacking in all areas of society. We are lacking in educational circles, the political arena, our families, out communities, and most importantly, the church. A good example of men lacking is this Sunday – look in your church service. You will find that our sisters three to one outnumber us. Our men are disappearing from the forefront. Men, our search for faithful men is going to have to take us to God. You might ask this morning how do we reach our fellow brothers? How do we develop faithful men? God can show us the answers. At the Church of God in Christ we are asking God to show us his hand this year. We have to enlist together as men of the church and begin to pray and fight to the best of our ability to develop faithful men. I have to tell you this, men there are a lot of sisters out there "waiting to exhale" because they haven't experienced a faithful man. A lot of men out there today are trying to look stylish; some men are out there looking like they came out of GQ magazine, but I'm here to tell you this morning that stylish doesn't mean faithful. There are a lot of men who can quote scripture backwards and forwards, but being in church and quoting scripture doesn't make you faithful.

The greatest need in the black community is a faithful man. I need you to know that I'm not talking about being faithful to your woman. You can't be faithful to your woman, to your family, to your job, to your children, or to your church until you learn to become faithful to God. Men, in order to be an asset to your people, you are going to have to learn to be faithful, and to have faith in God.

When we begin to look at the 11th chapter of Hebrews, or as I like to call it, the chapter of the hero's of faith. When we look at this epistle, it is being written to a group of men and women who were being persecuted but remained faithful and were justly rewarded. I need you to grasp some basics today. It doesn't matter how loud we shut in church or how often we come to church; my bible teaches me that without faith it is impossible to please God. Our focus has to be on pleasing God. When we try to please other people, we will find ourselves in a mess. As a matter of fact, I preached on that not long ago. "How did I get myself in this mess", how many of us can testify as to being in a relationship where we tried to please constantly please someone, and after doing everything that we could possibly do to please them, we find that they still aren't satisfied. Our best wasn't good enough. I've been telling you some dos and don'ts today, but I need you to understand some basics about this thing called faith. I want to get into some word today to tell you how to develop into a faithful man. The word says he that cometh to God, must believe that God is. It doesn't say that God exists; even old slew foot, the devil, believes that God exists.

This is where the faith factor begins to kick in. We have to believe that God is. He's just not on Sunday morning, or on a Saturday Morning Prayer breakfast, but God is all week long. He's not just God when everything is all right, but God is God when we are up and when we are down. He is God when you are sick and when you are in good health. He is God when you are broke, or when your pockets are fat. God is God whether you are saved or not saved. Men, the key is to believe that God will reward your faithfulness. He's a way maker, He's Jehovah Jireh, the God who will provide, and He is Jehovah Shalom, a God of peace. He is Jehovah Ropha, a God who heals. As a matter of fact, God is my all and all.

Can I have a witness by someone who has been sick and God has been your doctor? Can I have a witness today that God has filled your refrigerator when you didn't have any money to buy food? Is there anyone who has had his or her heart broken and God put it back together? Is there anyone here today who has had a problem that you couldn't solve, and God was your problem solver? I'm here to tell you that God is real, and He will reward you when you are faithful. I am not just talking about a rewarder of money or things that you can see. If I were just talking about material things, you wouldn't be here today. God breathed the very breath of life into your nostrils this morning. If God wasn't a rewarder of faithfulness, you brothers wouldn't be looking so good this today. We wouldn't have been able to eat that fine breakfast we enjoyed. God is a rewarder, He rewarded us with a sound mind, peace, joy and power this morning. I need you to know today that God just doesn't reward anybody. He doesn't reward you because you sit on the Deacon's bench, or you're in the puppet ministry or even because you may be sitting in the pulpit, but

He rewards you because of your faithfulness. I may not be able to see how you are going to get out of a certain situation, but God sees and knows all. Have you ever been in a situation where you couldn't see your way out? You were at your wit's end, you didn't know how you were going to make it, but you just trusted the Lord? Good God can I get a witness? Didn't He do exceedingly and abundantly above all that you asked or even could conceive that He would do? I'm a living witness this morning of how God rewards faith and faithfulness.

When we look at the word, we can look at some great men who exuberated great faith. Look at Abel when He offered a more excellent sacrifice that Cain. He gave and offering by faith. We can look at Enoch who walked with Christ for 365 years. Look at his faith; He walked with somebody he couldn't even see. The bible tells us that because he walked with God as he did, he pleased God.

To develop into a faithful man, we have to focus on pleasing God, not pleasing people. Let's look at the 5th and 6th verses of Hebrews. It says that Enoch was translated that he should not see death, but before the translation he had a testimony. His testimony was that he pleased God.

Men I ask you, can this be said of you? Do you live your life to please God? Can the people you work with tell that by the way you carry yourself? Would they say that your primary job description is to please God? Oh my brothers, what about your children, they way you treat them? Would they say that your life is geared toward pleasing God? Look beside you today, would the person sitting next to you say that your primary mission in life is to please God? Can they say this by the way you act, they way you speak, they way you worship, the way you act in private? As Christian men, do we separate ourselves from the world? Let me let you in on a little secret. When you please God, you can please your wife, when you please God, you can please your children. The first thing first, we must learn to please God.

I would like to tell you about some of the things that separated these heroes of faith in the epistle of Hebrews. They held beliefs that others didn't hold. They held their beliefs no matter what; some were murdered for their belief. Some were put out of work and some were crucified. The writer of this great epistle was letting us know that only men of great faith can make it through these difficult times, times like we are facing today. Men, we are persecuted for our beliefs, we struggle within our own government, we struggle with discrimination, and we struggle with our employers just to name few. Yes, we have a struggle today, but we have to realize that we cannot overcome without faith in God.

We can look back at history and look at some of those old-timers. Our grandmothers and grandfathers could do more with a little bit than we can with a whole lot today, just because of their faith. They stood on God word; they didn't have anything else to stand on. We need to get back to a time were we are solely dependant on God. It is faith, not education or money that makes the difference. It is faith, not an afro-centric name, which makes a difference. The issue today is how do we develop men of faith? How do we become faithful?

First, we have to define what faith is; verse one in Hebrews gives us our definition. Faith is the substance of things hoped for and the evidence of things not seen. If you can see it or touch it, you don't have to have faith in it. Faith means believing in that which you do not see, that which you cannot touch, that which you cannot experience with your senses. Faith means believing it to be so anyhow.

113

Faith does not believe that you are going to get something, but faith believes that God, whom one cannot see, is so real that if God said it, if God promised it, then it will be. You will achieve it. Faith says that I may not have a job, but if I put my trust and faith in God, He will supply all my needs. I may not see it, but it is so.

My brothers, faith is the substance of things hoped for, and the evidence of things not seen. You got to know what faith is. Faith is not positive thinking, but faith is a gift from God, which is rooted in his essence. When you believe in God, you can say God is my strength and my redeemer. He is my way maker. I want you know that God does not reward me because I am your servant of minister. God does not reward me because of my education, but God rewards because of those who diligently seek him. In the mess that we are in today the Lord need soldiers who are willing to stand on the principles of His word. The Lord needs men who can withstand the fire and the storm of criticism. He needs soldiers who are confident that the Lord we serve is able to deliver them when they are faithful! God is able. I know that He is able. There is no valley too wide for Him to cross. There is no road too tough for him to walk. There is no hunger too great for the Lord to satisfy. There is no burden too heavy for Him to bear. Oh my brothers, will you pick up the bloodstained banner with me, and run on with me to see what the end will be?

In closing this, the Lord needs us to have faith and to be faithful with our endeavors in serving Him. My Brothers, will you seek the kingdom of God and His righteousness with me? Let me close just by remembering the faith of Jesus Christ of Nazareth. In the 12th chapter of Hebrews in the 2nd verse, the scripture reads; looking unto Jesus the author and finisher of our faith. Who for the joy that was set before him endured the cross, despising the shame, and is set down at the right hand of the throne of God. Take with you the faith that Jesus had when He laid down His life so that we may have everlasting life.

Ask yourself, am I willing to be faithful and endure the criticism? Am I willing to set myself apart? All you have to do is pray a little prayer with me, my brothers. It a simple prayer, just pray Lord use me.

THE KING LIVES

SCRIPTURE: MATTHEW 28:1-7, 19, 20

Before going into this message I want you to be in prayer, just like Jesus instructed the disciples in the garden of Gethsemane. It is the key to overcoming any warfare.

A lot of prayer, A lot of power, some prayer, some power; little prayer, little power, no prayer, no power!

On Friday, they murdered my Jesus, or at least they thought they were murdering the King. I'm here to tell you that no man or woman could kill Jesus. He lad down His life on His own accord that He might take it again. No man can take Jesus' life. He laid down his life. I can't stress this enough. Jesus said, "That I have power to lay it down, and I have power to take it up again". Jesus laid His life down for the remission of our sins; God commissioned it a long time ago. God so loved the world the He gave his only begotten son, that whosoever believeth in Him should not perish, but have everlasting life.

It is my goal to give you an account of what the master went through, because of his love for you and I, so that we could be with

Him in heaven. He went through some excruciating pain. As a matter of fact I could not possible describe the pain with mere words. The word excruciating is derived from crucifixion. It comes from the agony and pain that one would endure if they were crucified. The derivative excruciate come from the Latin derivative "from or out of the cross". Jesus was beaten and flogged thirty-nine times; the skin was striped from his back, exposing a bloody mass of muscle, bone and tissue. His back looked like raw hamburger meat. He was then stripped naked and then a scarlet robe was put upon his torn skin. A crown of thorns was then pressed into his head. The roman soldiers had begun to torment and mock him saying, "Hail the king of the Jews". They began to spit on Jesus. On top of all this when Jesus looked around those closest to him had deserted him. After beating Jesus beyond recognition, He was led through the streets carrying a cross that weighed between eighty and one hundred and ten pounds. Do you know that He still bears that cross for us today and we won't carry those little toothpicks that we call burdens a couple of feet without wanting to quit. Christ bore that heavy cross almost six football fields long after being severely beaten. The cross was put on the ground and Jesus was laid on it, nails about seven inches long with a diameter of a centimeter. We would know this today as a spike or a 3/8-inch nail. These spikes were driven into his wrists. They would enter into the median nerve, which would cause excruciating pain to radiate through his arms. Standing at the crucifixion would be upright posts called Stipes, standing about seven feet high. In the center of the Stipes was a crude seat, called a Sedulum, which gave some support to its victim. The cross would then be lifted onto the Stipes. This allowed for the knees to be bent; The Kings feet were then nailed to the Stipes. The cross would then be lifted high into the air. This made it difficult for Jesus to breathe. They were slowly suffocating him. Every time His body would get weary and would slouch down to rest, the position of his body would make it difficult for him to breathe. He would have to push His body up with His feet, which were nailed to the cross. Man has no idea of the severe anguish and torment that his body was suffering. He was slowly being suffocated by his own body weight. Before Jesus laid down his life, which He gave up on his own accord, He called out with a loud voice "Father into your hands I commit my spirit". Remember this is just an overview of what Jesus endured for you and I. Words could never describe what actually happened.

Jesus wasn't murdered He endured the cross to fulfill His destiny. He knew all of this would occur. Scripture after scripture tells us that this was His destiny. Psalms 22:16-17 says, "Dogs have compassed me, the assembly of the wicked have enclosed me, they pierced my hands and feet".... Jesus knew the torment and pain He would suffer. He allowed this to happen, because of his agape love for us. In our struggle in life we need to remember that His love will conquer all. Isaiah summed it up for us in 53:5 when he said, "God was wounded for our transgressions, he was bruised for our iniquities, the chastisement of our peace was upon him and with His stripes we are healed". Jesus fulfilled his mission when He came, died and rose on the third day that we might live.

The word of God goes on to tell us that on the third day the two Mary's had approached the tomb toward the end of the Sabbath. There was a great earthquake and the angel of the Lord descended from heaven. The angel rolled back the stone and sat upon it. Scripture tell us that his countenance was like lightning and his raiment was white as snow. The guards were scared and they began to shake, they became as dead men. I can imagine how scared they were. They were ready to flee. The guards had become helpless in the presence of the angel. They were ready to run away. The angel told the women not to be afraid. He told them he knew they were seeking Jesus. It's something about seeking Jesus, it seems you can be easily separated from the rest of the world when you seek the face of Jesus. When you seek the Lord you don't have anything to fear. It's when we aren't seeking Jesus that we should be afraid. If God be for us, who can be against us? We are under the protection of the Almighty. The angel told the women; Jesus is not here He has risen. We serve an awesome God. In no other religion has the leader ever risen from the dead. If you go to Mecca you will find Elijah Muhammad still there, but if you go to Jerusalem Jesus will be gone. As a matter of fact some of those other religions such as Buddhism, you can just knock those statues or symbols right off the wall. I don't know about you but I don't want to serve a god that can be knocked off a bookshelf or one that collects dust.

I want you to know that our Jesus, our God is alive and well today. Because our King lives death has no more sting, because the King lives the grave has no more victory.

Because the King lives, we can overcome cancer, we can recover all that we have ever lost; because Jesus is alive and well we can overcome any obstacle or trial in life. All we have to do is seek and we shall find, knock and the door shall be answered. Because the King lives today we have power. We don't have to take the devils mess in this warfare of live. We can submit to God, resist the devil and command him to flee our lives in the name of Jesus. Because Jesus lives somebody like you and me can come out of the mire-clay. God can take someone hooked on drugs and alcohol and mold them into a positive, productive member of society. He can change a person in the twinkling of an eye, if they answer the knock. The knock is when Jesus pounds on the door to your heart. If you let God in things will change in the twinkling of an eye for you.

Because Jesus lives when we have a need we can begin to cry out Jehovah-Jireh and He will provide. When we are having an inner-struggle we can cry Jehovah-Shalom and he will command peace on our behalf. When disease has plagued our bodies when can call out Jehovah-Ropha and He will heal. All because of Jesus lives we can conquer any conflict that we have in our body or mind, as long as we seek Jesus. When things begin to be too much for us we can abide in the secret place of the most high, He will shield us with His shadow. Because the King lives we can fight a good fight, we can lay hold onto eternal life all because Jesus endured the cross for you and me. Because the King lives we can face tomorrow, overcome the past, and know that today He has given us a gift called the present.

Scripture tells us that after they had found that the King was no longer in the tomb, and that death had no more dominion over Him we were given the victory through our Lord and Savior Jesus Christ. Now that you know the King lives, you have some duties. Some of you have been called for a special assignment in the army of the Lord. I can hear Him choosing some of you to a higher call. Just like when He was calling the disciples. I can hear the Lord saying, " Oh not you, but you Zebedee, but I'll take your two sons James and John. I can hear the Lord calling some of you for special duty. Are you ready? I can here the lord saying I'll take you the tax collector. I can hear the Lord, can you? I hear Him; I'll take you the Physician. God has something special He is calling each of us to do, will you accept the call and endure the challenges of life? He has called each of us to go out and teach all nations, baptizing them in the name of the Father, the Son and the Holy Ghost. The question is are you going to pick up the bloodstained banner and live a righteous life. You as a Christian have been called to a higher way of life. Live Holy and with integrity, don't let anything hinder you from the truth. The key to this battle in life is to be all that God has for you, and don't let the world hinder you. If you do this you will be able to recognize Jesus when He comes to you. If you live holy and are sanctified and filled with the Holy Ghost you will recognize the voice of the Lord when he speaks to you.

The next time you are in a struggle remember all the torment Jesus suffered for you and I. Remember how badly he was beaten so that you could have life. He wants you not only to have life, but also to have it more abundantly. I can hear Jesus telling you to deny yourself pick up the cross and follow Him. I can clearly hear the Master saying, "I am the resurrection and the Life, he that believeth in me, though he were dead, yet shall he live, and whosoever shall believeth in me shall never die, Believest Thou This"? I leave you with this question Do you believe that God can restore you to the place you were predestined to be?

Conclusion

It has been my goal to equip you for warfare. I have told you where I was, how I got there and most importantly how God delivered me. This is my testimony of how God delivered me from mine iniquities. I want to arm each of you with some scriptures that I use on a daily basis. If you haven't learned anything from my life story know this; that it is God's intent to deliver everyone on this earth to salvation and when it looks like there is now way out God has already created an escape. Take these scriptures and fight a good fight. Be blessed in the name of the Lord!

For the LORD thy God walketh in the midst of thy camp, to deliver thee, and to give up thine enemies before thee; therefore shall thy camp be holy: that he see no unclean thing in thee, and turn away from thee.

Deut 23:14 (KIV)

Many *are* the afflictions of the righteous: but the LORD delivereth him out of them all.

Psalms 34:19 (KJV)

And call upon me in the day of trouble: I will deliver thee, and thou shalt glorify me.

Psalms 50:15 (KJV)

He shall deliver thee in six troubles: yea, in seven there shall no evil touch thee

Job 5:19 (KJV)

The Lord knoweth how to deliver the godly out of temptations, and to reserve the unjust unto the day of judgment to be punished:

2 Peter 2:9 (KJV)

And the Lord shall deliver me from every evil work, and will preserve *me* unto his heavenly kingdom: to whom *be* glory for ever and ever. Amen.

2 Tim 4:18 (KJV)

Call To Discipleship

If at any time during the reading of this book, God has touched your heart and you want a new way of life, just drop to your knees and confess your sins and accept Jesus Christ as your personal savior. Then find yourself a church home. God is able and willing to restore your life. Don't fight the battle yourself. God has already paid the price for your sins. If you need prayer or would like for Elder Perry to speak at your next church or business function. He can be reached at 1-866-War-Dept or you can visit him on the web at www.thewardepartment.com

About the Author

From a small town to the kingdom of heaven, Elder Jan-Dennis Perry rose from the grips of the devil to his rightful place with God. This reformed drug dealer/addict has turned his life around and is on a mission to save souls. He has weathered many storms to be able to stand before you today with a testimony all his own. Taste for a moment his trials and tests and know the wondrous works of the Lord. He is a simple man with a great love of God. Take a look and see how God has brought him from the fierce streets of society into a refined, well- educated servant of the most High! Today Elder Perry holds a Bachelor of Arts Degree from Marshall University and is pursuing a Master of Science Degree in Industrial and Employee Relations. In the corporate world he is known as a skilled leader and expert salesman. He is the winner of Verizon Communications highest sales award, "The Presidents Club". He is a known motivator and skilled coordinator in both the Corporate and Christian Community. Elder Perry has put on educational symposiums at major universities and small organizational gatherings. He is analytical skills are visionary. His marketing skills have been used to increase membership in the Christian Community and productivity in the Corporate World. His primary goal is to Empower people and declare war on Negative Attitudes!

CPSIA information can be obtained at www.ICGtesting.com
Printed in the USA
BVOW02s2046040915

416623BV00002B/242/P